The
Heart
of
Change
Field Guide

The Heart of Change

of

Change

Field Guide

Dan S. Cohen

HARVARD BUSINESS SCHOOL PRESS

Boston, Massachusetts

Library of Congress Cataloging-in-Publication Data
Cohen, Dan S.
    The heart of change field guide : tools and tactics for leading change in your organization / Dan S. Cohen.
        p. cm.
    Includes index.
    ISBN 1-59139-775-8
    1. Organizational change. I. Title: Tools and tactics for leading change in your organization. II. Title.
    HD58.8.C622 2005
    658.4'06—dc22

                                                                                    2005012861

The paper used in this publication meets the minimum requirements of the American National Standard for Information Sciences—Permanence of Paper for Printed Library Materials, ANSI Z39.48-1992.

To Corrie and Evan,

the pride and joy of my life,

who have taught me

the true meaning of change.

CONTENTS

PART II

Engaging and Enabling the Whole Organization

FOREWORD

In 1996, I published a book titled *Leading Change*. Based on work done over the previous decade, it examined why change efforts so often failed to live up to expectations. It reported common errors organizations made while implementing new strategies, adding new IT systems, reorganizing, acquiring and integrating other firms, or attempting to change their cultures. The book presented an eight-step pattern that illustrated and explained how some enterprises succeed while so many others fail to achieve their goals. The pattern starts with creating a sense of urgency and ends with institutionalizing change in the organization's culture.

Within three or four years, the book had achieved some notable success, but many of the people using the "formula" from *Leading Change* were asking for more advice and help. Deloitte Consulting suggested we jointly conduct additional research, with Dan Cohen acting as project head on the Deloitte side. We did so by sending a team of people to find concrete stories about significant organizational change efforts. Interviews were conducted in close to one hundred organizations from around the world. We published what we learned in 2002 as *The Heart of Change*—a book containing not only analysis but real-life stories reported by real people dealing with very real problems within all kinds of organizations.

More than any other single finding, we discovered in this second project that people changed less because of facts or data that shifted their thinking than because compelling experiences changed their feelings. This emotional component was always present in the most successful change stories and almost always missing in the least successful. Too many people were working on the mind without paying sufficient attention to the heart.

Two years later, we were told the *Leading Change* formula was being used by more organizations in North America than any other single change model. We were also told that additional concrete tools, tactics, and advice would be helpful. So, Dan and Deloitte launched a third project. This time they developed many practical methods, assessments, and diagnostics, based on their experiences in their own consulting assignments. The book you're reading presents those tools and represents a practical companion to the original two books.

The *Heart of Change Field Guide* takes the insights from the earlier research projects, adds a wealth of experience that the Deloitte people have had with many change projects, and translates all this into a deeper level of actionable material. It provides the reader with questionnaires to assess problems and challenges. It offers very specific issues a team needs to address. It's filled with checklists. It has a level of how-to that is much more specific than that of the first two books.

It is hard for me to believe that anyone coping with change, and most certainly anyone who has read the original books, cannot find something here of clear and substantial value. In some ways, this book is like a thesaurus or dictionary for a writer. You don't use all of it all the time, but it is an essential companion.

Since the vast preponderance of evidence says that the rate of change will only continue to increase, it is also hard to conceive that the tools in this field guide won't be even more helpful five years from now.

—John Kotter
Cambridge, Massachusetts
January 2005

Leading Organizational Change

Change remains the crucial challenge for organizations. Since *The Heart of Change* was published in 2002, I have traveled around the world talking with leaders about changes they are making in their organizations. Universally, they tell me that the pace, amount, and complexity of change only continue to increase, with no sign of letting up. They also admit that successful change almost always requires more of their time than they anticipate. In fact, a number of them indicated that during a major change effort, they spend upwards of 40 percent of their time focused on the initiative. Moreover, when we discussed the emotional side of change, they wholeheartedly agreed on the vital role that emotional investment plays, not only during implementation but also in sustaining the change for the long haul.

During our discussions, leaders told me that the flexible framework of the eight steps in *The Heart of Change*, as opposed to a more conventional, rigid approach, helped them in planning and designing their change programs. The real-life stories offered as a part of each step also helped them to really *see* how emotions help in successfully navigating change. Many suggested that a guide offering templates as well as diagnostic tools to help them structure their approach would be invaluable in bringing the eight steps to life.

This guide is intended to help anyone involved in or planning a change effort to design an initiative that utilizes the eight steps of change. It can be viewed as the third installment of the eight-step change process introduced by John Kotter in 1996 with *Leading Change* and followed by *The Heart of Change* (John Kotter and Dan Cohen) in 2002. The intent of the prior two books was, first, to introduce the eight steps and then to offer real-life examples of how the steps have been applied in organizations. This "field guide" is meant to go even further, to provide readers with the concrete tools, templates, advice, and insights for successfully achieving lasting change in their own organizations.

The *Field Guide* is literally meant to be a *guide*, not a workbook. With its many questions, diagnostics, and frameworks, it's meant to help individuals and teams plan and execute a change by providing insights into the process of change rather than a detailed recipe. It should be used as a catalyst to provoke thoughtful discussion and action that will ensure the success of a change initiative rather than be seen as a rigid set of procedures and practices.

A Systematic Approach to Leading Organizational Transformation

Before going into greater detail about how this guide can be used, it may be useful to provide an overview of the eight-step model for change. The model suggests that successful change is most often achieved by following a rolling eight-step process. Our additional field work and research at Deloitte has shown that these eight steps may be usefully grouped into three major phases in a transformation: (1) creating the climate for change, (2) engaging and enabling the whole organization, and (3) implementing and sustaining the change. (See figure I-1 for a visual representation of the model.)

FIGURE I-1

Eight-step process for leading successful change

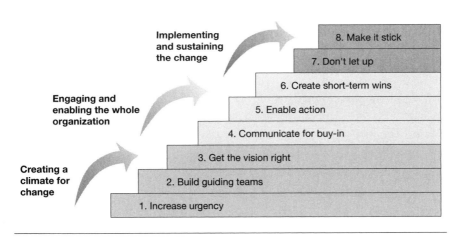

Creating a Climate for Change

The first phase involves building the needed level of energy to get the change off the ground.

1. Increase Urgency

In this first step, change leaders must build a sense of urgency about the needed change by heightening energy and motivation. To do this, they will need to reduce the fear, anger, and complacency that may have built up in their organizations.

2. Build Guiding Teams

The next step is to mobilize leaders who are focused, committed, and enthusiastic and can lead the change because they:

- Have a deep understanding of the why, what, and how of the change.

- Model the "right" behavior.

- Hold both themselves and others accountable for results.

3. Get the Vision Right

Step 3 involves creating a clear, inspiring, and achievable picture of the future. The vision must describe the key behavior required in the future state so that strategies and key performance metrics can be created to support the vision.

Engaging and Enabling the Whole Organization

The second phase is all about getting all of the stakeholders involved in the change by demonstrating leadership.

4. Communicate for Buy-In

During this phase, change leaders must deliver candid, concise, and heartfelt messages about the change in order to create the trust, support, and commitment necessary to achieve the vision.

5. Enable Action

In this step, leaders must bust the barriers that hinder people who are trying to make the vision work by developing and aligning new programs and designs, and by identifying processes that are ineffective.

6. Create Short-Term Wins

During this step, leaders must reenergize the organization's sense of urgency by achieving visible, timely, and meaningful performance improvements to demonstrate that progress is occurring.

Implementing and Sustaining the Change

The final phase is centered around insuring that the change is lasting by leaders being tenacious.

7. Don't Let Up

This step is critical to ensure that the guiding teams are persisting, monitoring and measuring progress, and not declaring victory prematurely.

8. Make It Stick

In this final step, leaders must recognize, reward, and model the new behavior in order to embed it in the fabric of the organization and make the change "the way we do business here."

The Nature of Change and the Eight Steps

A few key principles govern the use of the eight-step model:

- *Every step is necessary.* Each step in the process establishes a solid foundation on which to build change. Therefore, few change efforts will progress very far if any one of the steps is omitted.

- *The process is dynamic.* Although the preceding statement may suggest that creating change is a linear process, large-scale transformation is never that straightforward. The process of change is, by nature, dynamic. As a result, the change process might start in the middle, with creating a team or establishing a few short-term wins in order to boost urgency. Alternatively, it may be necessary for leaders to increase urgency (step 1) while also enabling action (step 5) and creating short-term wins (step 6) to energize the organization and create the climate for change. Short-term wins are also essential for creating credibility and momentum so that the organization is totally engaged in the change.

- *Several of the steps can happen simultaneously and continuously.* Some steps, such as communicating or increasing urgency, are typically executed continuously during the change process to generate the energy needed to make the change a reality.

- *Change is an iterative process.* The change process frequently requires retracing steps in order to successfully move forward.

Some steps, such as building a sense of urgency or creating guiding teams, will be revisited several times in the course of a transformation.

Two Approaches to Change

As illustrated in *The Heart of Change*, two approaches generally can be used in change efforts: *analysis-think-change* and *see-feel-change*. The work that led to that book showed us, however, that changing behavior is less a matter of giving people *analysis* to influence their thoughts than it is helping them to *see* a truth that will influence their feelings. Both thinking and feeling are essential, and both are found in successful organizations, but the true heart of change is in our emotions. The flow of see-feel-change is more powerful than that of analysis-think-change.

Table I-1 compares these two approaches side by side. Understanding the distinctions between analyzing and seeing is critical because, for the most part, in the business world we use analysis-think-change much more frequently, competently, and comfortably than we use see-feel-change. Shifting our focus to the see-feel-change approach takes a very conscious effort.

Using This Field Guide

Each of the eight steps described inspires change by speaking to people's emotions. This field guide offers guidance, approaches, and tools to lead change by gauging what the people in the organization see and feel. By design, you will not see many methods here that involve analyzing statistics. What you will see are systematic approaches to addressing people's fears, concerns, anger, complacency, excitement, or motivation. This is what this guide is all about: helping you keep urgency and energy up so that resistance stays down. If

TABLE I-1

Two approaches to change: logic and emotion

Analysis-Think-Change	See-Feel-Change
1. Give people analysis.	**1. Help people see.**
Information is gathered and analyzed, reports are written, and presentations are made about problems, solutions, or progress in solving urgency, teamwork, communication, momentum slippage, or other key problems within the eight steps.	Compelling, eye-catching, dramatic situations are created to help others visualize problems, solutions, or progress in solving complacency, strategy, empowerment, or other key problems within the eight steps.
As a result . . .	**As a result . . .**
2. Data and analysis influence how we think.	**2. Seeing something new hits the emotions.**
The information and analysis change people's thinking. Ideas inconsistent with the needed change are dropped or modified.	The visualizations provide useful ideas that hit people at a deeper level than surface thinking. They evoke a visceral response that reduces emotions that block change and enhances those that support it.
3. New thoughts change behavior or reinforce changed behavior.	**3. Emotionally charged ideas change behavior or reinforce changed behavior.**

Source: Reprinted with permission from John P. Kotter and Dan S. Cohen, *The Heart of Change: Real-Life Stories of How People Change Their Organizations* (Boston: Harvard Business School Press, 2002), 11.

the energy that urgency generates is not maintained, the effort needed to be successful in the other steps will fall short, and the fruits of the change will not be realized.

Whom is this guide meant to help? It is written for just about anyone responsible for or significantly involved in an organizational change effort. More specifically, by offering a framework for creating successful transformation, this guide provides guidance and tools to leaders, teams, and organizations:

- It supports and guides *leaders* of organizational transformation by defining a systematic approach for leading change and providing tools for evaluating the effectiveness of their change efforts.

- It provides *teams* working on change initiatives with practical guidelines on how to effect successful change.

- It offers *organizations* a consistent approach to leading change, in both language and method, that serves as a foundation for capturing and leveraging experiences from diverse initiatives within an organization.

The overall approach used in this guide has three distinguishing characteristics:

- It is *diagnostic.* It focuses on asking questions, offering suggestions and alternatives, and exploring potential challenges. This approach helps visualize problems, solutions, or progress in the change effort in order to affect people's emotions and evoke action. It is a framework to guide and support change leaders through important aspects of leading change.

- It is *scalable.* The approach can be used to lead organization-wide transformation as well as focused changes specific to a unit within the organization. It provides checkpoints that help leaders tailor the process to suit their needs.

- It is *flexible.* It can be tailored and adapted to reflect the unique aspects of each change initiative and each part of the organization.

The guide is best used to:

- Plan the approach for achieving each step in the change process.

- Identify what factors will enable or hinder the success of the change effort.

To increase effectiveness of the steps, integrate your use of this guide with other ongoing efforts that:

- Focus on communication throughout the entire change process.

- Attempt to capture the learning from both successes and failures to leverage your experience.

- Measure the progress of the change.

- Get constant feedback on your approach. Use a coach or colleague as a sounding board for new ideas and practices.

Chapter Structure

As in *The Heart of Change*, each chapter in the *Field Guide* describes a step in the change process. In the interest of providing an even more practical and hands-on guide to help implement the eight-step process, I've broken down each chapter into the following logical and easy-to-understand parts:

- *Purpose:* Defines the nature and aim of the step within the change process.

- *Approach:* Describes the key activities involved in the step.

- *Outcomes:* Identifies the optimal results of the step.

- *Key Implementation Challenges:* Explores the challenges that may emerge in the implementation of this step.

- *Gauging Effectiveness:* Provides a diagnostic tool for assessing the effectiveness of each step as it is implemented.

- *Suggestions for Improvement:* Suggests approaches for successfully navigating the step.

- *Communicating in This Step:* Defines the focus and challenges for communicating and getting feedback at each step.

- *Stories to Remember from* **The Heart of Change:** Provides challenging questions regarding change initiatives by referring back to some vivid stories from *The Heart of Change*.

- *More Resources:* Offers suggestions for where to learn more about the step.

Since this eight-step process is dynamic, and each step in this book is framed more or less as a self-contained module, feel free to turn directly to the step you are interested in reading about. If you have an interest in learning more about short-term wins before how to get your vision right, go straight to the section on short-term wins. If, however, you are coming to the eight steps for the first time, it makes sense to read the chapters in order so you can better understand the logic and cumulative power of the entire process. (In fact, read *The Heart of Change* and *Leading Change* as the natural and best introduction to the overall process.)

Now, on to step 1, increasing urgency!

ACKNOWLEDGMENTS

The *Field Guide* is the result of the work of many of Deloitte Consulting's current and past Change Leadership practitioners. In particular I would like to thank Lori Paschal, who spent many hours working with me on the *Field Guide* and whose suggestions and insights have proved invaluable. In addition, I would like to thank Jay Kacholiya, Andrea Heaberg, Gordon Cooper, Adriaan Jooste, Kelly Tompkins, Tammy Shaffer, Milt Hakel, Sid Chapon, Gerry Pulvermacher, and Ronnie Cohen as well as the editorial staff at Harvard Business School Press, led by Jeffery Kehoe, for their assistance in reviewing the manuscript and providing valuable comments, which assisted me in further organizing the guide. Finally, I would like to thank Mike Fucci, Jeff Schwartz, Doug Lattner, and Ainar Aijala for their support while the *Field Guide* was being written.

PART I

Creating a Climate for Change

A COMMON SCENARIO WHEN A LEADER OF an organization decides to undertake change is to begin planning immediately for the tactical implementation. Most leaders are quick to devote time, energy, and resources to redesigning new work processes or preparing new technology. However, little energy, if any, is spent getting the people within the organization ready for change.

Since the release of *The Heart of Change*, I have traveled around the world talking with top organizational leaders about transformation. Most agree that the most common reason their initiatives failed was that they did not address the people-related challenges—not that they didn't get the processes right or that the technology was not ready. If leaders acknowledge that projects fail for people-related reasons, why don't they do something about it from the beginning of their transformation effort? The answer is simple—it takes a lot of time and energy. So instead, they focus on the aspects that are more tactical and expect people to get on board. You've probably heard a leader say something like, "This is the direction we are going, and you just need to accept it and move on." Rarely does this approach result in lasting change.

This is why the first three steps are so important in the eight-step model—they work collectively to *create a climate for change* within an organization. Without a high degree of energy and urgency for change at all levels, the workforce will never embrace change, and lasting transformation will be harder, if not impossible, to achieve. By moving beyond the typical project steering committee to building multiple guiding teams in all levels of the organization, you create momentum and build commitment. Finally, the third step helps create a climate for change by providing a vision that people can rally around.

If you fail to create a climate for change, you are putting your transformation at risk. You give those individuals who choose to resist the change effort a solid platform from which to recruit others—people who would have been supporters if the proper climate had been set. Furthermore, even if the change is achieved, it takes much longer and is more costly in terms of both budget and effort.

To help you understand how to move through the first three steps, I encourage you to read the next three chapters, which focus exclusively on creating a climate for change within your organization. As you read these chapters, keep in mind that maintaining a climate for change requires you to periodically revisit the principles from these first three steps throughout the transformation to ensure that people do see and feel a supportive climate.

Increase Urgency

In successful change efforts, the first step is making sure sufficient people act with sufficient urgency—with on-your-toes behavior that looks for opportunities and problems, that energizes colleagues, that beams a sense of "let's go." Without enough urgency, large-scale change can become an exercise in pushing a gigantic boulder up a very tall mountain.

—from Step 1 of *The Heart of Change*

Purpose

To bring about significant change, an organization needs significantly more than the usual effort and commitment from its people. Everybody involved needs to believe that change is critical before they'll feel motivated to contribute to the effort. In addition, creating a clear sense of urgency around the needed change is crucial to gaining cooperation and sustaining the momentum of change.

But leaders are often tempted to skip this step. Creating a sense of urgency takes time and energy, and if the leader has already developed a concrete business case for the change, why bother? Our research and practice has shown us time and time again that while a concrete business case may be necessary, alone it is not enough to successfully change behavior; people first have to *see* and then *feel* the need to change. To change behavior, leaders need to know where any fear, anger, or complacency might have built up within the organization, and these emotions must be addressed in the approach to change. If they are not, the change effort will be in jeopardy of not making it out of the gate, and certainly the urgency needed to sustain the change will not persist in the later stages of the process. To jump ahead without the needed level of urgency is like trying to fly a plane without fuel. Do not make this mistake!

The dangers are partly built in. Being part of a large and successful organization may create complacency about the need for change and continuous adaptation to changing external conditions. People often make the natural and human mistake of believing that current preeminence in the market will ensure future success. Ford, Xerox, and IBM were successful leaders in their market for several years. It took a Toyota, Canon, and Microsoft to steer them toward major organizational transformation. To motivate people to change, organizations need to instill and maintain a sense of urgency about the difficulty of maintaining a leadership position in their market. In addition, employees need to see that change is not a one-time event but a continuous process of growth.

Approach

Generating a shared sense of urgency around needed change and adaptation requires three important steps:

1. Building a case for change that clearly identifies the gap between current organizational performance and desired performance.

2. Identifying the sources of organizational complacency.

3. Clarifying the roles of leaders and managers in implementing a change initiative.

Building a Case for Change

To gain initial support from top leadership, a case for change needs to be supported by a sound business rationale that is based on facts as well as on the probable consequences if the current situation is allowed to persist. This rationale can be created in a number of ways:

- Highlight performance gaps.

- Gather information about the organization's revenues, expenses, income, stock price, customer complaints, competitive situation, and employee morale and turnover.

- Develop clear indicators or measurements.

- Benchmark performance measures against the competition.

- Obtain powerful testimonies from important customers, employees, and shareholders who have left or are dissatisfied.

- Collect data about the organization's errors, failures, and missed opportunities.

- Gather information about trends developing in the market, the industry, or economy that contribute to the changing landscape of the organization.

However, a sound business case is not enough. The need for change has to be *seen* by people so that they can become emotionally charged to make things happen. This intertwining of logic with emotion is at the heart of successful change. To be compelling, the case for change must visually portray:

- *The situation:* facts and data about the organization's performance, the market situation, and the competitive position. The goal is to have people *see* the problem, solution, or progress in a compelling, dramatic way.

- *The problem:* the probable negative outcome if nothing changes—that is, what's at stake. The methods used must speak to people's emotions so that they can *feel* the problem.

- *The benefits:* the rewards and opportunities for change. People act on their emotions. Emotionally charged ideas *change* behavior and reinforce altered behavior.

Any new change initiative will lose momentum in the face of competing priorities unless the level of urgency around the change is clear, understood, and continuously reinforced through effective portrayal of the situation.

Assessment tool 1-1 was designed to help you identify elements that will create a solid case for change. While it begins with an analysis approach, it concludes by helping you assess ways you can link the change to emotions, thus enabling people to see and feel the need for change and increasing urgency.

Identifying Sources of Complacency

Increasing urgency means removing sources of complacency or minimizing their impact. The following list identifies some potential warning signs of complacency and suggests measures you can take to counteract it.

1. *No obvious, specific, and compelling rationale for the change effort that is shared by the entire organization.*
   Corrective action:

   - Highlight the precariousness of the current situation by drawing on examples of successful giants who lost their positions virtually overnight.

   - Articulate and stress the challenges of being the best.

   - Expose or remind managers of significant competitive weaknesses in the organization.

   - Communicate about errors instead of hiding them.

   - Reinforce the risks of settling for the status quo.

2. *Overuse of special benefits.* Corrective action:

Case for change worksheet

PERFORMANCE GAPS

What gaps have you had in performance? (e.g., revenue, expenses, stock price, customer service, morale, turnover)	How can you prove it? (e.g., existing data from metrics, research)

COMPETITIVE POSITION

Who are your top competitors in the marketplace?	What is your competitive position in relation to them? (e.g., revenue, expenses, stock price, customer service, morale, turnover, productivity)

ERRORS, FAILURES AND MISSED OPPORTUNITIES

What errors, failures, and missed opportunities have harmed the organization?	What did they cost the organization?	How do you know?

TRENDS

What market trends contribute to the need for change?	What industry trends contribute to the need for change?	What economic trends contribute to the need for change?

TESTIMONY

Whom should you contact to obtain powerful testimonies? (e.g., customers, current/former employees, shareholders, vendors)	What will you ask them?	How did they respond?

URGENCY FACTORS

What do people in the organization value?	What issues are causing fear, anger, and complacency?	What actions do you need to take to increase the level of urgency?

- Be fair but relentless in cutting down on excess rewards such as office size and location, personal and social benefits, travel advantages, and so on.

3. *Overall performance standards that are too low or relaxed.* Corrective action:

   - Set stretch targets that cannot be reached with business as usual.

   - Benchmark the targets against the competition.

4. *Organizational structures that focus people's attention on narrow functional goals (in other words, a failure to assign accountability for broad business performance).* Corrective action:

   - Start measuring people on "process" measures, not functional measures.

   - Measure performance on broad corporate objectives as opposed to narrow functional goals.

   - Help employees understand how their personal performance links to the overall performance of the business.

5. *Internal measurement systems that focus on the wrong performance indicators and control and planning systems that make goals too easy to achieve.* Corrective action:

   - Send more data about customer satisfaction and financial performance to more employees to demonstrate disturbing trends and weaknesses in relation to the competition.

   - Develop performance indicators that are more directly related to customer satisfaction and financial performance, and widely distribute and discuss.

6. *Performance feedback that comes almost entirely from internal systems.* Corrective action:

   - Insist that people regularly seek feedback from external sources, including dissatisfied customers, unhappy suppliers, disgruntled shareholders, and other dissatisfied stakeholders.

7. *A culture that avoids confrontation and kills the messenger.* Corrective action:

   - Force honest discussions in management meetings by using external sources to describe the problems.

   - Ensure that action items and decisions are recorded and identify an accountable individual.

   - Communicate integrity and organizational "safety" by encouraging open, constructive criticism in group discussions.

8. *A culture of denial. When managers are busy or stressed, it is human nature for them to ignore what they don't want to hear.* Corrective action:

   - Bombard people with information about future opportunities, the rewards for pursuing those opportunities, and the current inability to act on those opportunities. Eliminate deniability.

   - Drive home that "hope" is not a strategy; only action leads to successful change. Wishing will not make things happen, and ignoring a situation won't make it go away.

9. *Too much "happy talk" from senior management describing achievements based on past successes.* Corrective action:

   - Celebrate successes, but as a way to bring focus to the challenges and changes ahead.

   - Encourage discussions of the firm's challenges in newsletters and speeches.

   - Don't let people skim over tough issues in management meetings.

   - Always include the questions "What's going wrong?" and "What are we missing?" on the agenda at management meetings.

- Ensure conversations are solution-focused and not gripe sessions.

Clarifying the Role of Leaders and Managers

The primary role of leadership in this step is to make the need for change apparent to the entire organization—to make everyone involved *see* and *feel* the need for change. Leaders can accomplish this by:

- Taking ownership of the issue.

- Paying homage to the past while acknowledging the weaknesses of the present as well as the challenges of the future.

- Reaffirming that the market does not remain fixed by highlighting changes in an evolving business environment.

- Emphasizing the need for constant vigilance. Success yesterday does not mean success tomorrow.

- Communicating a compelling story and engaging all stakeholders in a dialogue about the need for change.

- Enabling managers to perform their change-related roles and responsibilities.

- Inviting ideas and suggestions for improvement.

- Coaching and mentoring other leaders in what it takes to be champions for change.

- Asking the hard questions and demonstrating courage.

If business unit/department heads have sufficient autonomy, they may be able to accomplish change in their own department or unit. But more often than not, change will cross functional boundaries and will require strong leadership support from higher levels. Therefore, the role of business unit/department heads is to take on the leadership role within their span of control by:

- Collecting information about the actual performance of their department or unit.

- Involving senior management in a serious examination of this information to gain support and commitment at higher levels for broader change.

- Taking the time to understand the true meaning of the change.

- Modeling the desired behavior to their constituencies.

- Holding people accountable for results.

Outcomes

The name of this step clearly communicates the desired outcome— increased urgency. Moreover, success in this step means gaining converts through both logic and emotion

- Gain *rational buy-in* by making a case for change based on solid data (financials, industry market trends, etc.), which provides a sound basis for confronting problems and measuring performance.

- Gain *emotional buy-in* by providing a compelling story or picture that catches people's attention and generates a high level of energy throughout the organization.

These two crucial attitudes or effects combine to generate the urgency needed to successfully launch the change initiative.

Key Implementation Challenges

Battling organizational complacency will likely be the most pressing challenge you face in increasing urgency around a change initiative. Here are some additional indicators of complacency:

- Significant issues are rarely discussed and never acknowledged.

- At meetings, problems are discussed, yet no decisions of importance are made.

- Decisions or suggestions are made but not acted upon; there is no execution or follow-up.

- Discussions of strategy are abstract and avoid confronting problems.

- Performance is mediocre, yet is praised by senior management.

- People are not asking questions, especially challenging ones.

- Leadership does not confront problems or is slow in making decisions.

- There is a "so what" attitude if things are not completed on time.

- People talk more about getting back to their "real job" rather than working on the initiative.

Gauging Effectiveness

Characteristics of an Increased Sense of Urgency

If you are effective at creating a shared sense of urgency, you'll likely see and feel it clearly, but here are just a few of the signs you might observe:

- Individuals challenging, questioning, and validating for themselves the need to change.

- More discussions and reiteration of the risks of the status quo.

- More talk about what's coming in the future; more long-term perspective.

- Greater awareness of the competition, the industry, and the external environment.

- Groups starting to investigate the source of the problems.

- More energy and effort directed toward satisfying customer needs.

In addition, use the following questions to help determine if the level of urgency is high enough to support your change effort:

- *How do your managers feel about the status quo?* Most companies can mobilize a change team and create a vision but find it difficult to engage the larger organization into action unless most managers honestly believe that the status quo is unacceptable.

- *Is the majority of the organization on board?* To sustain change efforts through implementation and beyond, a majority of employees, perhaps 75 percent of management, and virtually all of the top executives need to believe that considerable change is absolutely essential. The ultimate evidence of this belief is action, that is, what people do versus what they say they will do.

The Urgency Diagnostic

This diagnostic will determine the level of urgency that has been established in your organization. It will also reveal the potential obstacles you may face in establishing urgency. The following types of questions are included in the Urgency Diagnostic:

- *Questions about how your organization and its people operate and behave.* The word *organization* encompasses your whole company, not just your work unit. Questions regarding your specific work unit will be indicated as such.

- *Open-ended description questions.* At the end of the survey, you can offer suggestions on how your organization can raise urgency. Your views are extremely important in assessing the success of this first phase, so it is important not to overlook this portion of the diagnostic.

To use the diagnostic successfully, follow these steps:

- Distribute the urgency diagnostic form (assessment tool 1-2) to a cross-section of the organization to gather a broad-based view. Ask the individuals being surveyed to answer the questions according to their own experiences and knowledge of the organization.

- As indicated on the directions that accompany the diagnostic, respondents will assign a rating of 1 to 6 to each question, with 1 indicating "strongly disagree" and 6 indicating "strongly agree."

- Tally the results after the sheets have been returned to you. The farther the results are from the maximum score indicated, the more work that is needed on this phase of the change process.

The diagnostic should be confidential so those taking the questionnaire can be as open and honest as possible.

Suggestions for Improvement

If the scores are particularly low, you will likely have a problem establishing urgency around your change initiative. Furthermore, you may also need to watch for more general problems stemming from complacency, fear, and anger. Here are a few suggestions on how to address the problems that can block you from increasing urgency or that can lead to complacency, fear, and anger more generally.

The urgency diagnostic

Instructions

- Please read each statement and indicate the extent to which it describes the norm in your organization as a whole. Your responses should reflect what you have experienced as well as what you have generally observed in your organization.
- Answer the questions using a 6-point scale; the far left of the scale indicates that you strongly disagree and the far right of the scale indicates that you strongly agree. Please respond by checking the box that corresponds most closely to your situation.
- If you do not know the answer, check the "Do not know" box.
- Please take the time to respond to the open-ended questions at the end of the survey. Your responses are crucial in improving the change initiative.
- Be honest in your responses. There are no right or wrong answers, and your answers will remain completely confidential.

Sense of urgency	Strongly disagree (1)					Strongly agree (6)	Do not know
1. Our organization must change the way it works.	☐	☐	☐	☐	☐	☐	☐
2. My department must change the way it works.	☐	☐	☐	☐	☐	☐	☐
3. I need to change the way I work.	☐	☐	☐	☐	☐	☐	☐
4. The leaders of our organization seem committed to an immediate change.	☐	☐	☐	☐	☐	☐	☐
5. To stay ahead, we have to change.	☐	☐	☐	☐	☐	☐	☐
6. To get people motivated when undertaking a change initiative, leadership focuses on more than the "rational business case."	☐	☐	☐	☐	☐	☐	☐
7. Leadership really gets involved in leading change initiatives.	☐	☐	☐	☐	☐	☐	☐
8. We cannot stay ahead by continuing to work exactly as we do today.	☐	☐	☐	☐	☐	☐	☐
9. Leadership has shown us compelling evidence as to why we need to change.	☐	☐	☐	☐	☐	☐	☐
10. Leadership has shared outside information that supports our need to change.	☐	☐	☐	☐	☐	☐	☐
11. Leadership understands my job well enough to tell me to change the way I work.	☐	☐	☐	☐	☐	☐	☐
12. In the past, our organization has done a good job at change initiatives like this.	☐	☐	☐	☐	☐	☐	☐
13. Changes in this organization usually have a positive outcome for employees.	☐	☐	☐	☐	☐	☐	☐
14. I see a positive outcome for me as a result of this change.	☐	☐	☐	☐	☐	☐	☐
15. Leadership takes the time to create a sense of urgency before starting the change initiative.	☐	☐	☐	☐	☐	☐	☐

Subtotals   x 1   + x 2   + x 3   + x 4   + x 5   + x 6

= Grand total

(continued)

The urgency diagnostic *(continued)*

To get your totals

Add the check marks in vertical columns to get subtotals. Multiply that total by the number at the bottom of each column. Then add the subtotals together to get the grand total.

Grand total: 15 = serious problems, 90 = no problems. Any score below a 60 indicates a need for improvement.

Open-ended feedback

1. Do you feel a sense of urgency to change? Why? Why not?

_____
_____
_____
_____
_____

2. What would motivate you to take part in the change initiative?

_____
_____
_____
_____
_____

3. How will this change improve the organization?

_____
_____
_____
_____
_____

4. What risks do you see in this change?

_____
_____
_____
_____
_____

5. What could leadership be doing to demonstrate that this change effort is critical to the long-term success of the organization?

_____
_____
_____
_____

6. What would interfere with your desire/ability to take part in the change initiative?

_____
_____
_____
_____
_____

Bring the Outside World In

Organizations often get too inwardly focused and incorrectly assume that "our way is the best (and only) way." Bringing in outside data on competitors, the industry as a whole, or your customers' viewpoints can help focus the organization's attention on the changing world around it. This may come in the form of benchmarking data, customer surveys, market analysis, or, even better with regard to a see-feel-change approach, a visit to a competitor's site. Whatever the form, the information needs to *show* how your organization could benefit or how it's at risk. A good place to do this is at annual and semiannual leadership meetings.

Change or Improve Information Systems

A lot of you may be saying, "we already have benchmarking data," or "we already know what the customer thinks." But if urgency levels are low in your organization, then this information is not getting the right point across. It is supporting complacency by proving, over and over again, that your performance is just fine. Make sure that the data you are analyzing is the right data needed to drive change, and that the entire organization is receiving the information. If your change initiative is aimed at improving customer satisfaction, for example, but you focus only on the percentage rate of orders filled, you are getting only one piece of the equation. You may fill 100 percent of orders, but still have unhappy customers—perhaps they want orders filled faster. In order to get the entire organization involved, consider bringing in other data points to raise urgency. Spotlight areas that the organization struggles with to show the necessity for change. Don't just discuss the rate of orders filled at the executive steering committee meeting; include it in department meetings, e-mail alerts, and department newsletters. Have customers validate both efficiency and effectiveness measures. Now is not the time to be complacent!

Demonstrate Competence

If your organization is struggling with fear in particular, show employees that there is enough leadership competence behind the effort to make it a success. Often fear and anger are a result of past failures: "Last year, our company tried three different transformations and none of them worked. All they did was waste my time, my department's time, and our company's budget." To combat this type of fear and anger, you need to provide tangible evidence of what you will do to make this transformation different. For instance, refer to past successes, such as the revamping of the purchasing department in a matter of months. Then, focus on how that was only one win. Show the organization that you can carry this initiative forward with the same competence exhibited in the purchasing turnaround. This will turn the fear, anger, and cynicism from past failures into urgency around the new initiative.

Show That Your Interests Lie in the Greater Good

Talk about the future of the company and how it will benefit every employee. These types of discussions, more focused on the broad mission and coupled with the visible, concrete signs of competence just mentioned, will prove to everyone in the organization that your focus is in the right place and that you're capable of achieving the goal you've set.

Communicating in This Step

Even more than in all the other steps, communicating well is integral to increasing urgency. The following key points illustrate the most important aspects of communication in this stage of the change effort:

- Information must be first directed to the people at the center of the change process, to raise awareness and gain their buy-in.

As the change effort progresses, communication needs to be broadened to reach everyone involved in or touched by the changes.

- Awareness must be raised about issues and problems on a regular basis to constantly demonstrate the need for change and thus sustain commitment.

- The need to change must be continuously communicated by relating it to external market conditions and performance indicators, not just internal problems, dynamics, and potential benefits. The external reality is often the most powerful lever.

- Often, when lower-level managers communicate about changes to their group, the original messages are lost or disconnected from the market reality. These managers also need to present a strong imperative to change.

- Leaders and managers need to maintain open lines of communication and use "one voice" regarding the need for the change effort.

Stories to Remember from Step 1 of *The Heart of Change*

In *The Heart of Change*, John Kotter and I introduced many real-life stories, told by people from all kinds of business contexts, that vividly exemplified the eight steps in action and showed how integral the see-feel-change dynamic was in making change happen. I include a few summaries of those stories, focused on the important themes for each step, along with some questions to help clarify the critical role emotions play in successfully navigating change.

"Getting the Bosses' Approval"

After presenting a logical business case and gaining executive approval for implementing new enterprise systems across the organization, Ted Watson encountered barriers once the project was under way. Division leaders resisted, claiming the project would take too long, the cost-benefit was not strong enough, they could not operate without their resources assigned to the transformation team, and so on. While they wanted to decrease costs, division leaders fought any disruption to the business. As resistance grew, Ted was forced to stop the project and start from the beginning, which proved to be much tougher the second time.   (Summarized from *The Heart of Change,* pages 16–17)

- Do you face a similar risk of having to go back and redo things because people are saying "that's not how we run our business"?

- Do your key leaders and/or department leaders lack a sense of urgency around the change, or do they just not have the boss's approval?

"The Videotape of the Angry Customer"

Tim Wallace listened as one of his customers expressed frustration with his company's products and services. As Tim listened, it dawned on him that most of the staff who filled the orders never saw the customer at all, so he sent a small team to videotape the customer as he described his concerns and needs. Tim showed the video to groups of employees and led discussions to find long-term solutions to the problem so they could meet the customer's needs. Tim used videotaping in other situations to help the employees see the need for change and appeal to their emotions, which helped the plant transform to a customer-focused organization.   (Summarized from *The Heart of Change,* pages 18–20)

- How could videotaping a customer or an unhappy vendor help you?

- How could either help build a sense of urgency for your change effort?

"Gloves on the Boardroom Table"

Jon Stegner saw the need to make significant change to the company's purchasing process and calculated potential savings to be greater than $1 billion over five years. To help top leadership understand the enormity of the issue, Jon asked a summer intern to conduct a study on the cost of different types of gloves purchased by the factories. The intern found that the company was buying more than four hundred different types of gloves, and each location had its own supplier and negotiated price. As the division presidents came into the boardroom for a meeting, they saw the conference table piled high with gloves, each tagged with price and factory name. The presidents were awestruck as they realized for the first time how much they were spending on an item as simple as a pair of gloves without having a standardized purchasing process and vendor list. The glove demonstration became part of a road show within each division and in multiple plants, which helped establish a strong sense of urgency and a case for change. (Summarized from *The Heart of Change,* pages 29–30)

- Do your key leaders really understand the best practices the other departments use in issue handling, lead management, marketing campaigns, and so forth?

- Could some departments be paying far more for an equivalent service, media, or production of collateral than others?

"The CEO Portrait Gallery"

Pictures of past CEOs hung in the lobby for over a hundred years until Ron Marshall, the current CEO, took them down. They were meant to pay homage to great leaders and visually demonstrate continuity, but most regarded them as a shrine to former leaders, and they created an "us versus them" environment. In their place, Ron hung inexpensive pictures of the company's customers' stores. This caused quite a stir in the company, and the workforce began paying less attention to the past and more on the customers and their needs.

(Summarized from *The Heart of Change,* pages 31–33)

- How often has your organization hung onto out-of-date traditions in the name of "maintaining continuity"?

- How could doing away with such traditions drive new behavior?

- How could you use such an event to drive a sense of urgency?

More Resources

Bardwick, Judith. **Danger in the Comfort Zone: From Board Room to Mail Room—How to Break the Entitlement Habit That Is Killing American Business.** New York: AMACOM, 1991.

> Bardwick discusses the challenge of complacency in today's organizations—a complacency that has led to a continuing decrease in productivity and morale. She suggests that creating a strong sense of urgency is necessary to jolt us out of our comfort zone.

Bennis, Warren G. **Why Leaders Can't Lead: The Unconscious Conspiracy Continues.** San Francisco: Jossey-Bass, 1989.

> Bennis explores the current state of leadership and analyzes the difficulties impeding anyone who tries to take charge of an organization and overcome inertia. New insights are offered for change agents struggling to cut through bureaucracy and the status quo.

Chopra, A. J. **Managing the People Side of Innovation: 8 Rules for Engaging Minds and Hearts.** West Hartford, CT: Kumerian Press, 1999.

> An organization can unleash a powerful source of motivation in people by using their ideas to create change. This book will greatly increase the success of anyone charged with fostering innovation.

Eisenhardt, Kathleen M., and Brown, Shona L. "Time Pacing: Competing in Markets That Won't Stand Still." **Harvard Business Review**, March 1998.

> In this **HBR** article, Eisenhardt reveals how successful companies deal with rapidly changing, intensely competitive industries. Using a different approach she refers to as "Time Pacing" allows these organizations to create a relentless sense of urgency and concentrate people on a common set of goals.

Goleman, Daniel. **Working with Emotional Intelligence.** New York: Bantam Doubleday Dell, 1998.

> Being a successful leader of change requires a high degree of emotional intelligence. This book provides guidelines for enhancing self-awareness, self-confidence, and self-control as a foundation for increased commitment, ability to influence, and ability to initiate and accept change.

Goss, Tracy, Pascale, Richard Tanner, and Athos, Anthony G. "The Reinvention Roller Coaster: Risking the Present for a Powerful Future." **Harvard Business Review**, Nov. 1993.

In this **HBR** article, the authors present insights from companies that have successfully reinvented themselves by creating something entirely new rather than just changing what already exists. Reinvention includes assembling a critical mass of stakeholders to do an organizational audit, create urgency, harness contention, and engineer breakdowns that reveal weak spots.

Kim, Chan, and Mauborgne, Renée. "Tipping Point Leadership." **Harvard Business Review**, April 2003.

To accomplish the difficult task of engineering a corporate turnaround, executives must first break through addiction to the status quo by getting key managers to experience the organization's problems firsthand.

Ruettgers, Michael, and Hemp, Paul. "Managing for the Next Big Thing: An Interview with EMC's Michael Ruettgers." **Harvard Business Review**, Jan. 2001.

In this **HBR** interview, CEO Michael Ruettgers discusses how EMC has been able to anticipate and exploit disruptive technologies, market opportunities, and business models ahead of its competitors. Through processes such as quarterly goal setting and monthly forecasting meetings, EMC has maintained a strong sense of urgency that has allowed managers to get early glimpses of market changes and act on them.

Tobler, Adam. "How to Take a Strategic Approach to Implementation." **Harvard Business Review**, Feb. 1998.

Tobler outlines an approach for turning a winning strategy into a reality by garnering the support of top management, assembling the right team for the project, keeping the focus squarely on achieving the goal, building urgency around that achievement, and finally, leading for results.

Build Guiding Teams

A feeling of urgency helps greatly in putting together the right group to guide change and in creating essential teamwork within the group. When there is urgency, more people want to help provide leadership, even if there are personal risks. More people are willing to pull together, even if there are no short-term personal rewards. But additional effort is necessary to get the right people in place with the trust, emotional commitment, and teamwork to do the job. That's the step 2 challenge.

—from Step 2 of *The Heart of Change*

Purpose

You can't do it alone. No one can. Successfully achieving your change objective takes more than one individual or even one team. Significant change needs a number of powerful guiding teams who can actively champion the effort and take the necessary action when the effort comes up against barriers. Effective guiding teams not only have the credibility to influence stakeholders at the grassroots level, but also to engage and guide the organization through the change itself. Without strong guiding teams, change initiatives seldom have the support, energy, speed, and sense of urgency needed to succeed.

Approach

Creating guiding teams that work requires three critical elements:

1. Engaging the right people.

2. Setting clear team goals.

3. Developing a climate of trust and commitment within the teams.

Engaging the Right People

Key Roles

The size and composition of teams created to lead change initiatives will obviously vary depending on the nature of the proposed change. However, an effective structure for guiding significant organizational transformation must always include the following key supporters.

- *The sponsor:* The sponsor is typically a senior executive in the organization and the person who is ultimately responsible for the change initiative. This person's role is to provide executive-level support and the resources needed to drive the change effort. The sponsor also chooses the members of the senior guiding team.

- *The senior guiding team:* The senior guiding team is composed of individuals who have sufficient influence and authority in their area to make decisions and assemble the resources and support needed to make the change succeed. This team, which should be assembled at the very beginning of the change initiative, is responsible for developing the vision, engaging and guiding the organization during the change process, and managing the change initiative to its successful completion. It is important to differentiate a senior guiding team from a steering committee, which is more commonly found in organizations. Rather than a committee designed to approve recommendations and periodically review progress, the senior guiding team is a group of leaders actively involved in developing and implementing the change strategies. They are responsible for setting the strategy, providing the necessary resources, removing roadblocks and obstacles, clarifying priorities for the change teams, communicating with stakeholders, building support, and resolving conflicts. Large change efforts may require multiple senior guiding teams.

- *Field guiding teams:* The field guiding teams should comprise highly respected and credible people who are representatives of the constituencies in the organization that have a significant stake in the change. The role of the field guiding teams is to roll out the vision by engaging and guiding the organization in the change process as well as lead the change initiative to its successful completion. These teams will be established as the change takes shape and communication by credible leaders is required.

- *Change teams:* The change teams are composed of managers and supervisors who can ensure that tasks are completed properly and on time, and can provide assistance in the design and deployment of the change program. Change teams are formed when the tasks associated with the change are determined.

Although executive sponsorship and the development of an effective change team are important pieces of any transformation, it is the creation of the guiding teams, composed of strong leaders, that will ensure the success of the change. For this reason, the design and effectiveness of guiding teams is our primary focus for the rest of this section.

Skills and Attributes of Strong Guiding Teams

For guiding teams to succeed, the members must be people who have the necessary knowledge, perspective, and commitment to

TABLE 2-1

Key skills and attributes of guiding team members

Skills and attributes	Considerations
Power and influence	Which senior resources need to be part of the guiding teams for the change to succeed?
	Are representatives from each of the major stakeholder groups affected by the change included on the guiding teams?
	Can they sufficiently influence others in the organization?
Leadership	Do the teams include enough good leaders to be able to drive the change process?
Diversity	Do team members represent a sufficiently wide range of perspectives and disciplines to be able to make good decisions?
Expertise	Do the potential members of the teams have the required expertise?
	If not, do they have access to others with the needed subject matter expertise?
Credibility	Are there people who should be on the teams by virtue of the respect and credibility they garner in the organization?

tackle the challenge. Table 2-1 outlines the key skills and attributes that guiding team members should possess.

An effective method for selecting guiding team members is to evaluate all potential candidates using a criteria model. When developing your model, begin by brainstorming the criteria that guiding team members should possess. Next, brainstorm a list of all potential team members. Finally, evaluate each potential member against the criteria. Assessment tool 2-1 offers a sample criteria model for selecting a guiding team member. I have put in eight necessary criteria for the sponsor of any significant change initiative, but feel free to add other criteria points specific to your particular change effort.

The Ideal Size for a Guiding Team

For the guiding teams to have influence, they must include enough members from each stakeholder group to gain the group's

Sample criteria model: selecting a guiding team member

	CANDIDATES				
Criteria	**A**	**B**	**C**	**D**	**E**
1. Capable of providing executive-level support					
2. Capable of securing the necessary team members for the initiative					
3. Capable of securing necessary resources (financial support, technology, etc.) for the initiative					
4. Respected by other executives and leadership within the organization					
5. Capable of motivating and inspiring the organization					
6. Capable of making difficult decisions, even when they are unpopular					
7. Possesses the authority to make decisions					
8. Capable of removing barriers that prevent progress					
9. Other:					
10. Other:					
Totals					

Rating scale: 1 = Never; 2 = Rarely; 3 = Sometimes; 4 = Usually; 5 = Always

support. However, a large team may not be nimble enough to make decisions in a timely and effective manner. A balance must be struck between the need to gather organizational influence and the need to have small, effective teams that can work together in a holistic manner. As a rule of thumb, a team of more than twelve people becomes unwieldy very quickly.

Importance of Diverse Viewpoints on the Guiding Teams

Leaders of the change initiative need to share the same values and motivation in order to support the effort. However, to develop a strong foundation for the initiative, consider including individuals on the guiding teams who initially are strong resisters to the change. They can help people to understand where the resistance stems from and ultimately to gain the support of resisters. This is very important and valuable to any change effort. Ideally, such critical-minded people can be a crucial reality check for the initiative. However, there is always a risk that these individuals may not become "change zealots" and may end up doing more harm than good. If a team member remains dead-set against the change and cannot be objective and constructive in thought and action, the person may need to be excused from the team if the change is to succeed.

Changing the Composition of the Guiding Teams

The composition of the guiding teams will inevitably shift during the course of the change effort. You may have to replace exhausted leaders or add members who have the expertise required at a specific phase or have more influence in particular areas of the business. A common mistake, however, is to replace senior members with more junior ones as soon as the vision is created. Although the leaders' involvement will evolve, sustained leadership and executive commitment throughout all steps of the change process is necessary for the change to succeed. Moreover, as the change effort grows and takes root, additional guiding teams will be formed to nurture the change and ensure that it becomes part of the organization's modus operandi.

Setting Clear Goals

Without a common understanding of their goals, guiding teams may waste substantial time, mired in debate and conflict. Being able to set and uphold clear goals requires five basic elements:

1. *A shared sense of purpose:* This "purpose" must be aligned with the organization's direction, and should be clearly stated and shared by all.

2. *Clear roles:* Individual roles must be mutually understood and accepted in order for all team members to work effectively toward specific goals. Roles should recognize individual strengths and clarify expected contributions from each team member.

3. *Effective team processes:* A team must monitor a host of processes in order to be effective—team meetings, planning, problem solving, decision making, conflict resolution, and process improvement cycles. Effective processes are responsive to change and innovation and help a team work together more efficiently to achieve their goals.

4. *Strong relationships:* Creating strong relationships involves balancing the individual values (for example, degree of commitment to open communication, ability to trust, approach to conflict, etc.) of each member. The relationships between team members must be clear and strong in order to pursue common goals effectively.

5. *Effective interface management:* The effectiveness of a team and its ability to achieve goals is strongly enhanced or hindered by how well it manages interfaces and relationships with other teams.

Table 2-2 will help identify the presence of these five elements.

Developing a Climate of Trust and Commitment

Trust encompasses both doing what you say you will do and performing the activity at a level that meets or exceeds the expectations of others. When trust is present among team members, you will see open and honest discussion, free of politics and self-interest. Teams that do not create trust cannot function together, and as a result, will produce results that are only as good as the best member. When trust is present, you can usually create teamwork . . . when it's missing, you can't. Beyond trust, the element crucial to successful teamwork

TABLE 2-2

Key team elements for achieving change

SHARED SENSE OF PURPOSE

Elements of an effective team	Considerations
Shared understanding of change imperative	Do all team members understand the need for change?
Shared understanding of purpose and mission	Is there a common understanding of the team's mission and purpose?
	Can group members answer the questions: Who are we as a group and why are we here?
Clear goals and objectives	Do team members understand what goals and objectives the team is trying to achieve?
Appropriate goals	Do team members agree that these are the appropriate goals for the team?
	Are there clear timelines in which the goals and objectives are to be achieved?

CLEAR ROLES AND RESPONSIBILITIES

Elements of an effective team	Considerations
Mutually understood roles and responsibilities	Do team members have clear roles and responsibilities?
	Does each team member understand his/her own contribution toward the achievement of the goal?
Mutually understood performance measures	Are the performance measures for team members clearly understood?
Shared understanding of risks and challenges	What are the main risks and challenges ahead?
	What is their likely impact on the change initiative?
	What is the likelihood of the change happening?
Shared understanding of critical success factors	What are the critical success factors?

TABLE 2-2

Key team elements for achieving change *(continued)*

EFFECTIVE TEAM PROCESSES

Elements of an effective team	Considerations
A clear method for measuring success	What will be the key indicators of success?
	How will the team measure them?
A clear method for measuring progress	What are the key milestones?
	How will progress be measured?
A clear decision-making process	What key decisions need to be made?
	How will the team make decisions?
	Who has the authority to make decisions?
A clear issues tracking and resolution process	Has the team developed a process for tracking issues that arise?
	Does this process clarify accountability?

STRONG RELATIONSHIPS

Elements of an effective team	Considerations
An ability to resolve conflict	Does the team acknowledge and openly discuss conflicts?
	Is there a process to resolve those conflicts constructively?
A clear commitment from members (e.g., time, resources, etc.)	Is there agreement with respect to the amount of commitment team members will devote to the effort?
Mutually accepted ground rules for participation	Are there agreed-upon norms of behavior for working on the team in order to support trust, openness, and participation?

WELL-MANAGED INTERFACES

Elements of an effective team	Considerations
Clear communication channels	Are there specific channels and procedures for communicating within the team and with other teams?
Clear integration points	Are there clear integration points?
	Have interfaces with other teams and initiatives been identified?
	Have responsibilities for integration been assigned?

is having a common goal . . . only when all the members of the guiding teams deeply want to achieve the same objectives does real teamwork become possible.

Outcomes

You know you've successfully completed step 2 when your guiding teams:

- Are composed of individuals who have sufficient power, influence, expertise, credibility, and leadership ability to drive the change.

- Share a common understanding of the change initiative goals and are clear about the roles and responsibilities needed to make the change succeed.

- Are built on trust with a strong emotional commitment to a successful implementation and a strong sense of working together as a team.

- Understand and effectively employ approaches that will maintain high performance.

Key Implementation Challenges

Challenges arise at every stage of the development of a guiding team. In the early stage of the change process getting the right people on each team is a key challenge. However, once you've got good people on board, raising their sense of urgency and keeping it at a high level becomes a crucial ongoing issue. And this is complicated when members transition on and off the teams. As the change progresses, additional challenges arise in keeping the guiding teams focused on not letting up as well as making new behaviors stick. To meet these challenges, a clear sense of mission must be sustained so that team leaders can internalize the true nature of the change and be able to talk about it in concise, candid, and heartfelt ways.

Getting the Needed People on Board

Not all of the desired candidates for a guiding team will want or be able to participate. Therefore, you should consider the following questions as you begin assembling your guiding teams:

- Who are the right alternative candidates? Are there smart up-and-comers with strong credibility in the organization who might be just as effective?

- Is the person really needed full-time? Can the person be involved on a part-time basis?

- Could the role be filled by someone outside of the organization?

- If workload is a problem for some candidates, could their current positions be filled by their subordinates or a temporary replacement?

- Are certain aspects of the change initiative more likely to appeal to the people you wish to include? If so, can they be highlighted to attract those candidates?

Transitioning People In and Out of Teams

Over the course of a project, membership in the guiding teams may change. Having a defined approach to introduce new members that reinforces the team's mission, objectives, roles, and responsibilities will help ensure that the team does not lose its focus as its membership changes, and that decisions are not undone or rehashed. One approach to transitioning members is to have a time overlap between when a new member joins and an existing member leaves the team. This period of integration gives the new member the opportunity to not just understand the norms of the team but to feel them as well.

Managing Conflicts

Conflict often arises during a team's day-to-day activities. An established process for dealing with conflict can help prevent disagreements from hindering team performance. When conflict arises it should not be allowed to fester. Get the individuals who are having the conflict to air the issue in an open forum where they can listen to each other and then generate options that could resolve the conflict. Once the options are identified, have them discuss the possible solutions and identify the merits of each. Finally, see if they are willing to adopt one of the options to resolve the conflict. The key way to resolve conflict is to get the issue out on the table so that it is visible. If the issue is not confronted, the conflict will fester and only become more difficult to resolve.

Battling Complacency

Complacency often occurs after the initial energy and excitement about the change wanes. Maintaining a high level of urgency is critical, however, and requires constant attention, especially among the guiding teams. A guiding team renewal workshop can be a valuable tool for breathing new life into a complacent team. Topics reviewed or discussed at such workshops may include:

- Project objectives and goals, and how the team has progressed toward them.

- Key risk areas and success factors, and the strategies needed to address them.

- Successes and lessons learned, with an action plan to revise practices and work processes accordingly.

- Startling statistics, dramatic situations, and personally meaningful scenarios of why the change is important to spark emotions and renew the sense of urgency.

Maintaining Commitment

A team will quickly lose its energy and productivity if members
lose sight of their initial commitment and motivation. Team renewal
workshops can help maintain commitment through revisiting the
specific reasons for undertaking the change effort and discussing how
the organization will benefit in the long run. In addition, clearly
defined roles, responsibilities, and accountabilities can further reinforce commitment to the change effort.

Dealing with Team Members Who Are Defiant

As mentioned earlier, it is often a good idea to include strong
change resisters on a team in order to understand where the resistance is coming from. However, persuading these people of the risks
of the status quo may drain too much energy from the rest of the
team. Furthermore, they may become a barrier that the rest of the
team must overcome before driving forward on any action. This is a
sensitive issue, and detractors should be dealt with carefully in order
to avoid resentment as well as a decline in productivity. Some sea-
soned advice:

- Listen to their concerns and have them generate solutions.

- Persuade them to at least try the change; then take action on
their constructive feedback.

- Have them research industry best practices to see what other
organizations are doing.

- Do not accept a complaint without a solution.

Gauging Effectiveness

Characteristics of Strong Guiding Teams

Your guiding teams are operating effectively, with clear goals and trust among their members, if they consistently:

- Stay on track regarding their approach and direction.

- Rarely need to revisit completed work.

- Have open and honest discussions about problems, issues, and progress.

- Use conflicts constructively.

- Make tough decisions rapidly.

- Communicate frequently and clearly.

- Are effective at resolving issues using all members' knowledge and input.

- Work in and engender a relaxed and enjoyable atmosphere.

- Allow members to function autonomously, are clear about their roles and responsibilities, and integrate well with the other guiding teams.

- Understand and believe in the importance and urgency of the change effort.

If any of the following warning signs appear more than once, it is an indication that some or all of the teams do not have the necessary skills and attributes, are not senior enough in the organization, or do not have the necessary respect of the stakeholders to lead the change effort successfully. Consider yourself warned if your teams:

- Cannot get the resources, information, and support to progress rapidly.

- Do not motivate and inspire others to participate in the change.

- Cannot gain the support and help of specific groups in the organization.

- Cannot get on the leadership's meeting agendas.

- Cannot get one-on-one time with key leaders when needed.

- Constantly need to consult experts to make decisions.

- Cannot make important decisions without a lengthy approval and review process.

- Do not have the confidence of other senior staff.

If a competent key senior leader cannot mobilize a set of guiding teams with the right mix of credibility, expertise, and leadership, it is a sure sign that the organization has little appetite for the change proposed. For the business to release its best people for a change initiative, it has to share the need and urgency for the change.

Gauging effectiveness at this step in the change process merits two different diagnostic tools: one to determine how the members of the guiding teams see themselves (assessment tool 2-2) and one to determine how the stakeholders in the change process view the guiding teams (assessment tool 2-3). The results from these two diagnostics should be compared. If the two scores differ significantly, it is possible that the stakeholders in the organization do not view the change leaders as being as effective as the leaders think they are, or vice versa.

The Guiding Team Self-Assessment Diagnostic

Every good change initiative needs to be driven by groups of influential, effective leaders. These groups, the guiding teams, help the organization understand why the change is needed and thus must be fully committed to the change initiative, well respected within the organization, and have power and influence. This team self-assessment tool will help you determine how leaders see their own behavior as guiding team members, and how that perception influences team success and progress toward defined goals.

To use the diagnostic successfully, follow these steps:

- Distribute the diagnostic (assessment tool 2-2) to the guiding team members whose perspective is desired.

- Ask the individuals being surveyed to answer the questions according to their own experiences and knowledge of the organization.

- As indicated on the directions that accompany the diagnostic, respondents will assign a rating of 1 to 6 to each question, with 1 indicating "strongly disagree" and 6 indicating "strongly agree."

- Tally the results after the sheets have been returned to you. The farther a respondent's results are from the maximum score possible, the more likely it is that the person may not be an effective team member.

The Guiding Team Assessment Diagnostic

For an organization to accept the mandates and direction of a change initiative that a guiding team has proposed, it is critical that stakeholders in the change process respect the authority and skills of the guiding team members. This tool will help you determine how stakeholders see the effectiveness of a guiding team.

To use the diagnostic successfully, follow these steps:

- Distribute the diagnostic (assessment tool 2-3) to the stakeholders whose perspective is desired.

- Ask the individuals being surveyed to answer the questions according to their own experiences and knowledge of the organization.

The guiding team self-assessment diagnostic

Instructions

- Please read each statement and indicate the extent to which it describes the norm in your organization as a whole. Your responses should reflect what you have experienced as well as what you have generally observed in your organization.
- Answer the questions using a 6-point scale; the far left of the scale indicates that you strongly disagree and the far right of the scale indicates that you strongly agree. Please respond by checking the box that corresponds most closely to your situation.
- If you do not know the answer, check the "Do not know" box.
- Please take the time to respond to the open-ended questions at the end of the survey. Your responses are crucial in improving the change initiative.
- Be honest in your responses. There are no right or wrong answers, and your answers will remain completely confidential.

Guiding teams	Strongly disagree (1)					Strongly agree (6)	Do not know
As a leader driving this initiative, I . . .							
1. Truly believe that there is a need for change.	☐	☐	☐	☐	☐	☐	☐
2. Really want to see a change for the better.	☐	☐	☐	☐	☐	☐	☐
3. Understand the long-term effects that this initiative will have on our organization.	☐	☐	☐	☐	☐	☐	☐
4. Understand how people's jobs will be affected as a result of the change initiative.	☐	☐	☐	☐	☐	☐	☐
5. Have committed resources to the initiative.	☐	☐	☐	☐	☐	☐	☐
6. Publicly demonstrate (by attending meetings, leading meetings, publishing thoughts, etc.) my commitment to the change initiative.	☐	☐	☐	☐	☐	☐	☐
7. Reward people for their commitment to the change initiative.	☐	☐	☐	☐	☐	☐	☐
8. Hold people accountable for the change initiative by following up with them to ensure progress is occurring.	☐	☐	☐	☐	☐	☐	☐
9. Have developed systems and procedures to measure the progress of the change initiative.	☐	☐	☐	☐	☐	☐	☐
10. Act as a role model by demonstrating the new behaviors required to successfully implement and sustain the change initiative.	☐	☐	☐	☐	☐	☐	☐
11. Feel we are working as an effective team.	☐	☐	☐	☐	☐	☐	☐
12. Keep employees informed on the overall progress of the initiative.	☐	☐	☐	☐	☐	☐	☐
13. Have power and influence within the organization.	☐	☐	☐	☐	☐	☐	☐
14. Am respected by both my peers and employees.	☐	☐	☐	☐	☐	☐	☐

(continued)

ASSESSMENT TOOL 2-2

The guiding team self-assessment diagnostic *(continued)*

Guiding teams	Strongly disagree (1)					Strongly agree (6)	Do not know
15. Trust my fellow guiding team members.	☐	☐	☐	☐	☐	☐	☐

Subtotals

= Grand total

x 1   + x 2   + x 3   + x 4   + x 5   + x 6

To get your totals

Add the check marks in vertical columns to get subtotals. Multiply that total by the number at the bottom of each column. Then add the subtotals together to get the grand total.

Grand total: 15 = serious problems, 90 = no problems. Any score below a 60 indicates a need for improvement.

Open-ended feedback

1. What are you doing to successfully contribute to the change initiative?

_____

_____

_____

_____

2. How have you involved other members of your organization in the change initiative?

_____

_____

_____

_____

- As indicated on the directions that accompany the diagnostic, individuals will assign a rating of 1 to 6 to each question, with 1 indicating "strongly disagree" and 6 indicating "strongly agree."

- Tally the results after the sheets have been returned to you. The farther the results are from the maximum score possible, the more likely it is that the stakeholder has a troubling lack of confidence in the guiding team in question.

Suggestions for Improvement

A single leader often heads up a change initiative, despite the danger inherent in this approach. A single driver cannot effectively handle

ASSESSMENT TOOL 2-3

The guiding team assessment diagnostic

Instructions

- Please read each statement and indicate the extent to which it describes the norm in your organization as a whole. Your responses should reflect what you have experienced as well as what you have generally observed in your organization.
- Answer the questions using a 6-point scale; the far left of the scale indicates that you strongly disagree and the far right of the scale indicates that you strongly agree. Please respond by checking the box that corresponds most closely to your situation.
- If you do not know the answer, check the "Do not know" box.
- Please take the time to respond to the open-ended questions at the end of the survey. Your responses are crucial in improving the change initiative.
- Be honest in your responses. There are no right or wrong answers, and your answers will remain completely confidential.

Guiding teams	Strongly disagree (1)					Strongly agree (6)	Do not know
The key leaders driving the change initiative . . .							
1. Truly believe that there is a need for change.	☐	☐	☐	☐	☐	☐	☐
2. Really want to see a change for the better.	☐	☐	☐	☐	☐	☐	☐
3. Understand the long-term effects that this initiative will have on our organization.	☐	☐	☐	☐	☐	☐	☐
4. Understand how people's jobs will be affected by the change initiative.	☐	☐	☐	☐	☐	☐	☐
5. Have my trust and respect.	☐	☐	☐	☐	☐	☐	☐
6. Publicly demonstrate (by attending meetings, leading meetings, publishing their thoughts, etc.) their commitment to the change initiative.	☐	☐	☐	☐	☐	☐	☐
7. Reward people for their commitment to the change initiative.	☐	☐	☐	☐	☐	☐	☐
8. Hold people accountable for the change initiative by following up with them to ensure progress is occurring.	☐	☐	☐	☐	☐	☐	☐
9. Utilize measurement systems and procedures to measure the progress of the change initiative.	☐	☐	☐	☐	☐	☐	☐
10. Act as role models by demonstrating the new behaviors required to successfully implement and sustain the change initiative.	☐	☐	☐	☐	☐	☐	☐
11. Are working effectively as a team to make this change a success.	☐	☐	☐	☐	☐	☐	☐
12. Keep employees informed on the overall progress of the initiative.	☐	☐	☐	☐	☐	☐	☐
13. Have power and influence within the organization.	☐	☐	☐	☐	☐	☐	☐
14. Are respected by both their peers and employees.	☐	☐	☐	☐	☐	☐	☐

(continued)

The guiding team assessment diagnostic *(continued)*

Guiding teams	Strongly disagree (1)					Strongly agree (6)	Do not know
15. Have prioritized all of the projects to ensure that the change initiative gets the attention it needs to be successful.	☐	☐	☐	☐	☐	☐	☐
Subtotals	x 1	+ x 2	+ x 3	+ x 4	+ x 5	+ x 6	
= Grand total							

To get your totals

Add the check marks in vertical columns to get subtotals. Multiply that total by the number at the bottom of each column. Then add the subtotals together to get the grand total.

Grand total: 15 = serious problems, 90 = no problems. Any score below a 60 indicates a need for improvement.

Open-ended feedback

1. What do you think the leaders driving this initiative are doing well? What could they improve?

_____

_____

_____

_____

2. Do you believe that the leaders driving this initiative are visible and accessible enough? If not, how can they improve their visibility and accessibility?

_____

_____

_____

_____

3. How would increased leadership involvement make you more supportive of the initiative?

_____

_____

_____

_____

the large-scale, fast-paced change required in today's business world. On the other hand, delegating the change initiative to a project team or task force that does not passionately believe in the initiative or is buried deep in the organization is just as precarious. These groups usually fail because they do not have the credibility, common vision, connections, formal power, or leadership skills to create change quickly and effectively. Therefore, improvements at this step in the change process usually revolve around making sure your guiding teams share the urgency, vision, leadership, and esprit de corps needed to drive the change initiative efficiently. The following are specific suggestions and reminders for how to ensure that your guiding teams are strong and successful in their mission.

Make Sure Your Guiding Teams Are Effective

As the change initiative grows, so does the size (or number) of the teams. What often begins as a single dominant, driving force quickly expands to multiple groups in the organization. These groups should have some sense of urgency and the capacity to handle the difficult work. In addition, the initial team must include people who function as leaders and are respected in the organization. As change progresses, however, effective guiding teams are often formed at lower levels. Those teams drive action within their units and need to have the same commitment to the change effort as the existing guiding teams. For this reason, it is critical that the guiding teams obtain feedback from the team members as well as the individuals they are leading. It is even more important that team members take corrective action based on that feedback so others can see that their comments are being taken seriously. Be sure that the appropriate measures are in place to monitor individual performance and, if needed, take swift action to correct any performance issues. Remember, the individuals in the organization who are going to have to change the way they do things are watching and determining if leadership is "really serious this time around." Don't give them reason to confirm their doubts!

Build Teamwork, Trust, and Commitment

When people are committed to a vision, they usually trust others who were part of the team that developed the vision. Trust among members of the guiding teams grows as they meet each other's expectations and perform at a level that demonstrates results. As the level of trust increases, so will the level of commitment to the change objectives. As trust and commitment grow, the degree of leadership alignment increases because leaders now have a deep understanding of the change effort; they now act as role models to people in the organization and hold themselves and others accountable for results.

Keep the Team Motivated

In large-scale change initiatives, keeping the teams motivated over a long period of time may be difficult. This is compounded by the fact that guiding teams are often very diverse in their makeup; the members represent different areas of the organization, which often have differing wants and needs. In any change endeavor, it is often too easy for people to argue that "if it ain't broke, don't fix it." The members of the guiding teams, although chosen for their motivation and common sense of urgency, are not exempt from this natural instinct when things get rough. To boost team motivation, both formal and informal communication are critical, particularly involving the overall vision for the change and the long-term benefits. Finally, meetings should stay focused, organized, and as short as possible, and should have a tone of excitement to energize members.

Communicating in This Step

It is critical for the guiding teams to communicate with the organization so that people can see leadership's focus on the change effort and leaders can candidly relate why the change is needed, what the future will look like, and most important, how the journey will unfold. Hearing these kinds of messages is critical to success. Following are a few important points to consider about communicating with the organization in this step of the change process:

- Are members of each guiding team taking responsibility for communicating the imperative for change whenever they have the opportunity?

- Is it clear to the people in the organization which key leaders are attached to the project and what roles they play?

- Have members of each guiding team taken the time to understand and respond to people's fears and concerns?

- Are members of each guiding team motivating and energizing people in the right direction?

- Who should announce and present the guiding team members?

- What are the unique messages coming out of this step?

- What communication objectives are sought in this step? Awareness? Understanding? Motivation for action? Commitment?

- What critical audiences need to be targeted?

- Has two-way communication been used wherever possible?

- What feedback is sought and from whom?

- What feedback is being received? What is not?

- How is future communication being altered in light of the feedback received?

Stories to Remember from Step 2 of *The Heart of Change*

Use the following story summaries and questions to help you build guiding teams.

"The Blues Versus the Greens"

When two companies merged, their leadership ordered them to play nice with each other. But even though they acted cordially, there was still a strong undercurrent of "it's us or them." Although they attempted to create a shared set of values and one culture, they were unable to talk honestly about their struggles. In a management meeting led by a respected facilitator, the facilitator realized that the root of the problem was the leadership. He reprimanded them for not speaking honestly to one another about their problems and for not looking at their own behavior. The second day of the meeting was drastically different as leaders began to voice their frustrations openly for the first time. This meeting was the start of the change from "blue and green management" to one leadership team. (Summarized from *The Heart of Change,* pages 38–41)

- How can you align leadership to foster a unified team spirit? Who should be part of the guiding teams and how many teams should initially exist?

- How can you defuse the perception that your initiative is being pushed down the divisions' or departments' throats by corporate headquarters?

"The New and More Diverse Team"

Tom Spector worked for a company that acquired smaller companies in order to grow, and much of their energy went into making the deal. When there were no other companies to acquire, they could no longer rely on this method of growth, as it was time to focus on internal processes and the customer. Much of the leadership struggled with this transition and did not find the work as exciting. Tom was asked to be on the COO's new operating committee, comprising representatives from every major function and level of the organization, and they had the opportunity to shape the future of the company. While the diverse viewpoints often required a great deal of discussion on issues, the group was able to devise fresh viewpoints, resulting in more viable solutions that were more widely accepted within the organization since every group was represented.   (Summarized from *The Heart of Change,* pages 43–46)

- Do you need to build guiding teams? Why? What skills are needed to be an effective guiding team member?

- How can you create new and more diverse guiding teams? What strengths should you look for in cultivating that diversity?

"General Mollo and I Were Floating in the Water"

Roland de Vries was tasked with leading a team of South African army officers, men who had previously been on opposing sides, in creating a vision, strategy, and implementation plan for merging seven armies into one national army. When the team had its first meeting, the fire in each person's eyes said all that was necessary about the level of trust in the room! Seeing this, Roland quickly sought to set the tone by saying that trust was critical to the team's success and that he would always speak the "truth" because he knew that if this behavior continued, it would only result in more serious roadblocks later. He started the second meeting by sharing the pressure he received the previous night from his commander to make the combined force change to be like his army. He continued by saying that he did not believe it was the right approach and explained the reasons he would not do it. As others began to share similar stories, they began making progress for the first time.

(Summarized from *The Heart of Change,* pages 50–53)

- Do some team members have their own agenda and resist new ideas? How can you build their trust?

- How can you create the emotional energy to overcome the war-like animosity toward change and build unity through common sacrifices?

"Meetings Down Under"

Ateam of fifty-five people, representing diverse geographic regions, was formed to lead an Australian company through change. While there was excitement in the first few meetings, the team made little progress because they skipped from issue to issue without ever fully discussing them or agreeing on how to handle them. The CEO decided it was time to change the format by focusing on only one topic per session. The first day of each session concentrated on issues and solutions, and the second day focused on the timeline and action steps as well as selecting the topic for the next two-day session. This approach worked well, and the change team was successful in transforming the organization.

(Summarized from *The Heart of Change,* pages 55–57)

- What critical issues need to be resolved before you can move forward?

- Which key guiding teams should you mobilize to drive the other teams?

- What can you do to assist leaders who seem helpless?

- What can you do so that guiding teams can move forward with building their teams?

More Resources

Collins, James C. **Good to Great: Why Some Companies Make the Leap . . . and Others Don't**. New York: HarperCollins, 2001.

> One of the key concepts Collins reveals in this book is the need to get the right people on the bus. Establishing effective guiding teams is largely about selecting the right members to join them.

Conner, Daryl R. **Managing at the Speed of Change: How Resilient Managers Succeed and Prosper Where Others Fail**. New York: Random House, 1992.

> In this work, Conner describes the patterns of change, his unique principles of resilience, and the imperative that managers actively lead the change process.

Duck, Jeanie Daniel. "Managing Change: The Art of Balancing." **Harvard Business Review**, Nov. 1993.

> In this **HBR** article, Duck presents change as a dynamic process that requires balancing the conversations between change leaders and those expected to make the changes. Managing these emotional connections through the Transition Management Team concept will help leaders and followers work together effectively to create their future.

Dyer, William G. **Team Building: Current Issues and New Alternatives**. Reading, MA: Addison-Wesley, 1994.

> Any large-scale transformation involves the creation and management of teams at multiple levels of the organization. The book discusses the major new trends, including self-directed work teams, total quality initiatives, and cross-cultural teams, and reviews the strengths and weaknesses of these new developments in team building.

Gottlieb, Marvin R. **Managing Group Process**. Westport, CT: Greenwood Publishing Group, 2003.

> This resource explains the facilitation process and tools to help anyone wanting to better understand how to work with groups, make decisions, solve problems, and build commitment.

Harrington-MacKin, Deborah. **The Team Building Tool Kit: Tips, Tactics, and Rules for Effective Workplace Teams**. New York: AMACOM, 1993.

> Building and managing teams effectively is a critical part of leading change efforts. This book explains how to define roles and responsibilities, select team members, encourage positive behavior, maintain control, and evaluate and reward teams.

Hunter, Dale, Bailey, Anne, and Taylor, Bill. **The Art of Facilitation**. Tucson, AZ: Fisher Books, 1995.

> The authors discuss the secrets of group facilitation as well as how to equip group members to take on this role themselves.

Kiser, A. Glenn. **Masterful Facilitation: Becoming a Catalyst for Meaningful Change**. New York: AMACOM, 1998.

> This book offers a systematic approach to facilitation to help teams articulate their purpose, determine desired results, and choose and apply the most efficient level of intervention to achieve organizational objectives.

Lencioni, Patrick. **The Five Dysfunctions of a Team: A Leadership Fable**. New York: John Wiley & Sons, 2002.

> A compelling fable of a new CEO faced with the challenge of uniting a team that is in such disarray it threatens to bring down the entire company. Throughout the story, Lencioni outlines a powerful model and actionable steps that can be taken to overcome the five dysfunctions that afflict many teams.

Weaver, Richard G., and Farrell, John D. **Managers as Facilitators: A Practical Guide to Getting Work Done in a Changing Workplace**. San Francisco: Berrett-Koehler, 1999.

Facilitation of groups and processes is a key skill for anyone leading a change effort. This guide describes a new model for facilitation that more effectively clarifies goals, manages group dynamics, builds new processes, and manages changes.

Get the Vision Right

In successful large-scale change, a well-functioning guiding team answers the questions required to produce a clear sense of direction. What change is needed? What is our vision of the new organization? What should not be altered? What is the best way to make the vision a reality? What change strategies are unacceptably dangerous? Good answers to these questions position an organization to leap into a better future.

Far too often, guiding teams either set no clear direction or embrace visions that are not sensible. The consequences can be catastrophic for organizations and painful for employees—just ask anyone who has suffered through a useless fad forced on them from above.

—from Step 3 of *The Heart of Change*

Purpose

A shared urgency for change may push people into action, but it is the vision that steers them in the right direction. In addition, you need the right people on the guiding teams to overcome obstacles and continuously champion the vision if you want to see it become a reality. A good vision offers a compelling, motivating picture of the future and serves several important purposes:

- It clarifies the general direction of the change by providing a kind of motion picture—a living, dynamic illustration—of the behaviors required for success at all levels.

- It helps identify the behaviors that must be encouraged as well as those that must be eliminated.

- In proportion with its clarity, it helps pinpoint the key performance measures that can determine the level of slack (the gap between the desired and actual performance that is accepted by leadership) that occurs during different phases of the initiative.

- It motivates people to take steps in the right direction, even if the action is not necessarily in their short-term interests.

- It helps coordinate the actions of people throughout the organization quickly and efficiently.

Once the right vision is fully embraced, a few key benefits begin to emerge:

- Senior management can communicate to managers without detailed directives or endless meetings.

- Employees can figure out what to do without checking constantly with their manager.

- Interdependent groups can work with some degree of autonomy.

Approach

The basic approach to this step in the change process involves four key phases:

1. Clarifying why a vision is necessary

2. Developing the vision

3. Analyzing the vision

4. Clarifying the role of the team developing the vision

Clarifying Why a Vision Is Necessary

You have developed a compelling rationale for why the organization needs to change. A senior guiding team has been formed. The members have articulated a good definition of the problem and the underlying issues, and have sculpted their specific goals and objectives for the change. Why do you need a vision? In terms of the see-feel-change dynamic, it allows everyone involved with the change to see the need in a way that is clear and motivating, even inspiring.

To be effective, the vision should be clear, challenging and achievable. It needs to describe an outcome that appeals emotionally to those who will be involved in making it happen. This doesn't mean, necessarily, that the vision will make them laugh or cry, but that it must make people *feel* either the positive possibilities or the risk of maintaining the status quo. Though the vision should ultimately be a simple statement, its development is not a simple process. A vision should merge comprehensive, fact-based analysis with creative insights. Such a blend of perspectives helps ensure that the vision is realistic, achievable, and inspiring; will move the organization in the right direction; and fits into the organization's corporate objectives. A vision that is off the mark is worse than no vision at all. It is both costly and dispiriting to discover halfway through implementation that the vision is not achievable or will not yield the desired results.

Developing the Vision

The process for developing a vision is both a rational and a creative exercise. Ideally, it should involve many people and their perspectives, as well as extensive data. Thus, it is often an iterative, rolling, and seemingly unstructured process. Use the following steps as a model:

- Develop the first draft in an initial session with members of the senior guiding team.

- Collect and analyze data regarding the need for organizational change, including not only quantitative data but also anecdotes, stories, physical evidence, video, and the like to validate or modify initial assumptions about the external marketplace and internal issues facing the organization. Formulate a new hypothesis about how the organization will differentiate itself in the future.

- Discuss primary findings of the analysis with key players and sketch the main elements of the vision.

- Identify key behaviors that will be needed from leaders and employees in order to achieve the change, along with behaviors that will need to be eliminated so that people begin to picture in their minds what the future looks like.

- Repeat the above steps, collecting more feedback and information and further refining the vision until the picture of the future becomes crystal clear; then the strategy necessary for implementation can be clearly articulated.

- Identify metrics to measure progress.

- Validate the vision and its implementation strategy with a broader audience, with the eventual goal of getting input from all the stakeholders.

Figure 3-1 illustrates the multiple factors at work in the creation of a vision.

Analyzing the Vision

A comprehensive, fact-based analysis will ensure the vision is built on a solid foundation. The analysis will also reveal information about

FIGURE 3-1

Building a vision

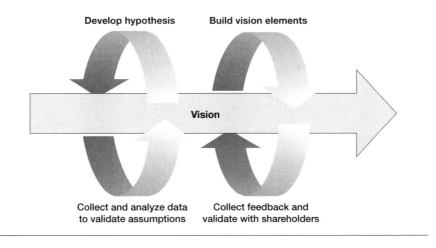

the size, scope, and scale of the change to come so as to align the appropriate resources for implementation. The process will involve:

- External assessment of the industry to determine trends in the competitive environment as well as the threats, opportunities, weaknesses and strengths facing your organization.

- Internal assessment to identify core competencies, key business processes and business performance

- Customer needs assessment to understand key requirements and expectations, drivers of satisfaction as well as issues and complaints

- Benchmarking to understand best practices and key metrics to measure success

Clarifying the Role of the Senior Guiding Team

The role of the senior guiding team in this process is to:

- Clearly outline how employees need to act in the future—things they should not do as well as those they should—for the change to be a success.

- Develop scenarios that will capture the imagination of stakeholders so they can see the opportunity for organizational growth.

- Obtain input from stakeholders throughout the visioning process.

- Communicate the vision to stakeholders in order to secure their buy-in.

Outcomes

You have successfully completed this step when you and your organization have:

- A picture for change that is compelling and focused, and helps everyone in the organization understand how their behavior contributes to the vision.

- A clear understanding of the behaviors that need to be added, removed, or maintained in order to achieve the vision.

- A sound strategy that defines how the vision will be achieved and demonstrates the feasibility of the goals.

- The foundation for determining the key performance indicators to determine success.

Key Implementation Challenges

Creating a compelling vision that describes where your organization wants to go, that shows your people the future in a clear and motivating way, can be difficult. Here are some reasons why.

Unfamiliarity with Visioning Activities

Creating a vision is very different from the normal managerial activities of planning, budgeting, and controlling a part of the business. It takes not only the ability to accurately analyze and assess the current context in concrete terms, but also the ability to imagine and communicate different possible futures. The individuals who create the vision must have the right knowledge, skills, experience, and imagination if a meaningful vision is to emerge.

Determining Behavioral Impact

Once the big picture is created, the team must determine how it will be "acted out," that is, the individual and organizational behaviors needed to realize the vision. This requires the team to think about how people at all levels must modify their behaviors in the future. Once the team has identified these ideal future behaviors, it then has to determine which current behaviors need to be encouraged and which need to be eliminated. This can be hard, tedious work, and team members often encounter resistance from others in the organization, not only to the time required to identify the many relevant behaviors, but also to implementing and following them.

Letting Go of the Past

Creating a vision for the future requires the ability to detach from years of traditions and habits as well as letting go of current pressing problems. The guiding team may be too tied to the past or too engrossed in the present to achieve this goal.

Answering the following four questions can help guiding team members to step back, get perspective, and create a clearer vision of the future:

- What will the organization look like once the transformation is complete?

- What will employees say about the organization once the transformation is complete?

- What will customers say about the changed organization?

- How will we measure organizational and individual performance in the future?

Incomplete and Complex Data

The final product defining the vision may be a simple document, but the data and analysis required to produce it are not. Data is often incomplete, complex, and not easily available. Forming a clear, coherent organizational (or unit) vision from a mass of different kinds of information requires not only imagination, but also focus and discipline. Don't let the detail overwhelm you or cloud your own vision.

Combining Head and Heart

Creating a vision cannot be just an exercise in assessing market and organizational opportunities. It must also reflect values that resonate with the leaders and everyone affected by the proposed change. Both rigorous data analysis and creativity are required in the process, as well as constant attention and sensitivity to the values and interests of the group.

Building Relationships

The goal of this phase is the creation of a sensible vision to which everyone in the organization is committed. However, unless people have had time to think, argue, feel, and reflect, they may have difficulty embracing the vision. Thus, the vision creation process requires more than a task-oriented approach. Leaders must focus on relationship development as part of the process, and should not expect to accomplish the goal in one meeting. In many ways, while developing the vision, the guiding team is also learning about themselves, their values and priorities, and how to work together. That process alone takes time and dedicated teamwork.

Making the Final Product a Living Document

The vision is not a static thing like a technical document or a portrait on the wall. It needs to be revisited and tweaked and updated when external or internal situations change or early implementation efforts highlight needed changes. This ongoing process will keep the vision vital and relevant. Also, it is important to communicate what gets changed and why to the whole organization to keep everyone on the same page and to avoid losing credibility.

Gauging Effectiveness

Characteristics of an Effective Vision

An effective vision is one that forwards the change process by being clear and easily understood. The vision must appeal to people's emotions so they can see and feel the need for change and are motivated to be part of it. An ineffective vision, one that does not achieve these things, is worse than no vision because it leads to wasted effort and destroys credibility for future change initiatives. At a minimum, an effective vision must be:

- *Futuristic:* Not a Jetsons scenario, but a clear, imaginable picture of what the future will be like.
    - ✓ Does it describe a future activity or group in a way that can be visualized?
    - ✓ Does it describe the future in terms that are meaningful and compelling?
- *Compelling:* Motivates people to action.
    - ✓ Does it help people understand why change is really necessary?
    - ✓ Is it ambitious enough to force people out of comfortable routines?

✓ Does it include innovative elements or radical new ideas?

- *Desirable:* Appeals to long-term interests of as many stakeholders as possible.

  ✓ Does it speak to current and future customers?

  ✓ Does it speak to a wide range of employees?

  ✓ Does it speak to stockholders and any others with an important stake in the organization?

- *Realistic and feasible:* Consists of realistic, achievable goals that can be measured. Stretches resources but is grounded in reality.

  ✓ Does the vision require stretching resources and capabilities to an extent that demands significant changes in the way business is conducted?

  ✓ Are the goals considered ambitious yet realistic and achievable with great effort?

  ✓ Can the vision be measured in concrete terms?

  ✓ Is the vision considered sound by those with a deep understanding of the organization, its market environment, and competitive trends?

  ✓ Does the vision take advantage of fundamental trends in the industry?

  ✓ Does the vision imply that some things should no longer be done?

  ✓ Is the vision consistent with the realities faced by the organization?

  ✓ Is the vision for this change consistent with the greater outlook for the organization?

- *Clear and focused:* Clarifies what's important. A clear vision can guide decision making and help to:

  ✓ Eliminate confusion as to the direction the organization is headed.

✓ Reduce the debates and disagreements on direction and move people to action.

✓ Identify inappropriate or tangential projects that can be terminated to free up resources.

- A vision is *focused* if it:

    ✓ Reduces the number of possible actions to what's feasible.

    ✓ Points to specific areas that need to change.

    ✓ Identifies key enablers for the change.

    ✓ States clear targets and planned results.

    ✓ Includes explicit statements about desirability.

- *Flexible:* A vision is sufficiently flexible if in the course of its implementation:

    ✓ It does not provide many directives that constrain individual initiative.

    ✓ It does not need constant readjustments to changing circumstances, which would affect its credibility.

- *Easy to communicate:* An effective vision must be clear, convey tangible benefits, and appeal at an emotional level.

    ✓ Is it clear enough that it can be successfully explained within five minutes?

    ✓ Does it make business sense throughout the organization?

    ✓ Can it be expressed in concrete terms?

    ✓ Is it achievable?

    ✓ Does it appeal to people's emotions?

The Vision Diagnostic

Individuals must understand the vision and its implications for how the organization will look and feel in the future. The Vision

Diagnostic will help you determine how well stakeholders understand the vision. In addition, it will tell you how stakeholders see the degree of change as well as its relevance.

To use the diagnostic successfully, follow these steps:

- Distribute the diagnostic (assessment tool 3-1) to individuals whose perspective is desired.

- Ask the individuals being surveyed to answer the questions according to their own experiences and knowledge of the organization.

- As indicated on the directions that accompany the diagnostic, respondents will assign a rating of 1 to 6 to each question, with 1 indicating "strongly disagree" and 6 indicating "strongly agree."

- Tally the results after the sheets have been returned to you. The lower the results are beneath the maximum score possible, the more urgent the problem.

Suggestions for Improvement

The vision is an essential part of a change initiative. Without a clear, motivating vision, efforts at organizational change can lead people in circles and result not only in decreased urgency, but in real losses of productivity and credibility. If the scores are low on the diagnostic, you should stop and reevaluate your vision. If the vision is not clear, concise, and feasible, you should not expect others in your organization to understand, believe in, or adopt the change initiative. Following are suggestions for how an organization can strengthen its vision.

Make Creating a Vision a Priority

There are many reasons why organizations have an inadequate vision or no vision at all, but a common one is that it's simply not a

The Vision Diagnostic

Instructions

- Please read each statement and indicate the extent to which it describes the norm in your organization as a whole. Your responses should reflect what you have experienced as well as what you have generally observed in your organization.
- Answer the questions using a 6-point scale; the far left of the scale indicates that you strongly disagree and the far right of the scale indicates that you strongly agree. Please respond by checking the box that corresponds most closely to your situation.
- If you do not know the answer, check the "Do not know" box.
- Please take the time to respond to the open-ended questions at the end of the survey. Your responses are crucial in improving the change initiative.
- Be honest in your responses. There are no right or wrong answers, and your answers will remain completely confidential.

Getting the vision right	Strongly disagree (1)					Strongly agree (6)	Do not know
As a member of this organization, I . . .							
1. Understand the vision that we are driving toward.	☐	☐	☐	☐	☐	☐	☐
2. Can explain the vision in five minutes or less.	☐	☐	☐	☐	☐	☐	☐
3. Can describe the behaviors that our leaders want to witness more often.	☐	☐	☐	☐	☐	☐	☐
4. Understand how the vision affects my job.	☐	☐	☐	☐	☐	☐	☐
5. Feel that the projects that are inconsistent with the new vision have been, or will be, terminated.	☐	☐	☐	☐	☐	☐	☐
6. Am motivated by the vision.	☐	☐	☐	☐	☐	☐	☐
7. Believe that achieving our vision will make us a better business.	☐	☐	☐	☐	☐	☐	☐
8. Can describe the behaviors that our leaders want to witness less often.	☐	☐	☐	☐	☐	☐	☐
9. Feel that the vision is flexible enough that it can be changed in light of changing market conditions or feedback from employees.	☐	☐	☐	☐	☐	☐	☐
10. Believe that our vision is feasible.	☐	☐	☐	☐	☐	☐	☐
11. Think that our vision takes into consideration our organization, the market environment, and competitive trends.	☐	☐	☐	☐	☐	☐	☐
12. See others trying to act more in line with the behavior implied by the vision.	☐	☐	☐	☐	☐	☐	☐
13. Believe that the vision is backed by sensible actions toward achieving our vision.	☐	☐	☐	☐	☐	☐	☐
14. Understand how these actions will help us achieve our vision.	☐	☐	☐	☐	☐	☐	☐
15. Believe that our organization has the skills necessary to achieve the vision.	☐	☐	☐	☐	☐	☐	☐

Subtotals

= Grand total

x 1   + x 2   + x 3   + x 4   + x 5   + x 6

(continued)

The Vision Diagnostic *(continued)*

To get your totals

Add the check marks in vertical columns to get subtotals. Multiply that total by the number at the bottom of each column. Then add the subtotals together to get the grand total.

Grand total: 15 = serious problems, 90 = no problems. Any score below a 60 indicates a need for improvement.

Open-ended feedback

1. What do you like about the vision? How do you think the organization could improve its vision?

_____

_____

_____

_____

_____

2. What don't you understand about the vision?

_____

_____

_____

_____

_____

3. How do you see the vision impacting your job?

_____

_____

_____

_____

_____

4. What would make you more supportive of the vision?

_____

_____

_____

_____

_____

5. What behaviors would you like to see more of to achieve the vision? What behaviors would you like to see less of?

_____

_____

_____

_____

_____

priority. Creating a vision is often put on meeting agendas, but is just as often ignored because "this week we need to focus on the decreasing market share problem" and "next week we must resolve the high inventory level problem." Vision is viewed as "soft" and not immediately connected to profits. An organization might recognize that change is necessary and take steps to implement it, but without a clear vision, the change initiative will be directionless and will likely stray from its intended path. It will also lack propulsion, the energy to keep moving forward. A motivating vision helps to boost urgency and maintain focus. To make the vision happen, you must gather several respected leaders who will make creating the vision their first priority—and then won't let up until the vision has the approval of all members involved and the collective buy-in of the other key guiding teams.

Keep the Vision Short, Simple, and Inspiring

A vision should inspire, challenge, and spark emotion and excitement. One big mistake is muddling the vision with plans or strategies. "Cutting costs by 5 percent" is not a vision, but rather a goal for achieving a vision. When a change initiative is in place, many people tend to justify the change by bringing in numbers and figures that document why the change is necessary. Then they incorporate these numbers into the vision statement—hardly exciting.

Another mistake is making the vision too long-winded. A great vision is one that is easily remembered and can be easily communicated to all members of the organization. A good vision should be short—it outlines only *direction*, not specific plans or strategies. A good rule of thumb is that if you cannot articulate a vision in a sixty-second elevator ride, you have a problem.

Support the Vision with a Strategy

In today's rapidly changing world, it is easy to shoot for the stars—to envision a radical organizational change that will produce drastic benefits and rewards. The strategy for realizing the vision should be equally radical. Many organizations create an exciting new vision, but when they begin to implement the strategy, they fail to develop the appropriate action steps and stick to old habits. It's no surprise they find themselves wondering why things haven't changed. A strategy should support and realize the vision, not hinder it.

Communicating in This Step

Getting the vision right is crucial to successful organizational change. Communicating that vision well is just as essential. Here are a few important points to consider about communicating during the vision development phase.

Increase Communication Before Developing the Vision

Another approach that has been used successfully by many large organizations, more in line with the process described in this guide, is to spend more time up front gathering input and developing key elements of the vision before the vision itself is drafted. (Again, see the more organic process illustrated in figure 3-1.) Relevant information can be obtained from many people simultaneously using large group interventions, and the vision can then be refined using smaller groups of experts.

Validate the Vision with All Stakeholders

Regardless of the approach chosen to develop the vision, the results need to be validated with a number of stakeholder groups to ensure the vision is realistic and feasible, and to identify the key challenges that will be faced during implementation. This process includes sessions where the vision, in its draft form, is presented and feedback is collected through a survey or questionnaire. To gain as many points of view as possible, feedback should be sought from various stakeholders, including:

- Leaders who will need to commit.

- Customers, suppliers, or stockholders.

- Management and employees from all parts of the organization who will have a role to play in the realization of the vision.

- Independent experts who have a solid knowledge of the industry and/or business strategy.

It is important that the documents presented be in a *draft format*. Participants are more likely to give honest feedback if they feel their input is going to help shape the next version, rather than being asked to agree to a final document. If the vision is in draft form, participants will also understand that what they are seeing is likely to change in the future.

Close the Loop

A common mistake is to request input and validation from several parts of the organization but fail to close the loop regarding the impact of their contribution. This oversight increases resistance later when additional input and support are needed from those same individuals. As soon as possible, explain what input has been incorporated in the vision, what has not been included, and why.

Maintain Constant Communication with Stakeholders

Because the process of developing and validating the vision may take some time, it is important to maintain dialogue about the change initiative to keep momentum.

- Educate the organization about the change initiative's progress using recent findings.

- Keep key stakeholders abreast of changes in the vision and the progress of the work.

- Don't wait until completion to present the vision to various leaders of the organization. Show them material as it evolves. Not only will they have a chance to provide input, they will also get time to reflect on it.

Make It Clear That Input Is Always Welcome

Regardless of the manner in which the vision is developed, it should never be perceived as an exclusive, privileged effort. Make sure the people in the organization know they can contact a guiding team with their ideas.

Checkpoint: Move Forward or Revisit Prior Steps?

Before engaging the organization, evaluate your success thus far in achieving an actionable vision and a solid foundation for change. The following are key warning signs that you may need to revisit some prior steps in the change process:

- A common sense of urgency is lacking due to an overlong process of developing and validating the vision.

- The senior guiding team:
    - ✓ Is not developing a compelling vision.
    - ✓ Is getting bogged down in endless negotiations and compromises.
    - ✓ Cannot convincingly communicate why the change effort is so critical, what the future looks like in concrete terms, or how the organization will make the transformation.

If these warning signs are present, you may need to revise the composition of the senior guiding team before moving forward.

Here are a few important points to consider at this stage:

- *Can the same individuals who created the vision implement it and carry it to completion?* The development of a vision requires strategic thinking, creativity, and deep analytical skills. While this type of leadership will still be required, after the vision is drafted consider adding individuals to the team who are good at building relationships, making the tough decisions, and producing results.

- *Do representatives from other parts of the organization need to be involved?* The vision may now define changes affecting parts of the organization that were not initially represented in the guiding team, but are critical to the success of the initiative.

- *Do members of the team have sufficient authority and credibility to accomplish the task ahead?* Is the composition of the team still consistent with the size and scope of the task?

Stories to Remember from Step 3 of *The Heart of Change*

The following story summaries and questions can help you determine if you "got the vision right."

"Painting Pictures of the Future"

With deregulation and liberalization of the U.K. market, this company realized it would have increased overseas competition, and also had the opportunity to expand through acquisition. The CEO started an "orthodox planning process" that resulted in continued discussion but no action a year later because no one understood the options and consequences. In order to move ahead, a team defined each key option in terms of the following dimensions: sales turnover, employees, customers, businesses, competitors, beliefs, and action steps. By painting a picture of the company's future for each option and refining each picture in a series of meetings, leadership was able to visualize each option and understand the scale of change required to make it successful. While data and financials were necessary for analyzing each option, it was the discussion stemming from the pictures that helped this company proactively create its future. (Summarized from *The Heart of Change,* pages 62–66)

- Do you have a clear picture of the future?

- Are you proud of the vision and can you align key leaders around it?

- How can you add more of the see-feel-change perspective to your vision?

- Which behaviors will demonstrate that you are living the vision?

- Which behaviors do you want to encourage? Which behaviors do you want to discourage?

- How will you measure performance toward achieving the vision?

"Cost Versus Service"

When Ron Bingham began a change effort within a state government, he shared the opinion of the governor that the vision should be focused on cost savings, a topic he knew would be met with resistance from the state employees, who felt they should serve the community at any cost. But when Ron changed the focus to customer service and clearly explained what that would mean for the workforce, they became inspired by the vision and believed they could truly improve the way they served the community. As the workforce began to examine opportunities for improvement within their areas, they supported changes wholeheartedly—even when it meant staff reductions, process changes, and so forth. As a result, the state saved more money than they ever deemed possible, allowing them to reallocate the funds to help them meet the community's needs.

(Summarized from *The Heart of Change,* pages 70–72)

- What are some of the ways you focus on cost versus service?

- What are some creative ways to get a service focus into your vision?

- Have you thought about why people *don't* purchase from your organization a second and third time? Are you making any of the cost versus service mistakes?

"The Plane Will Not Move!"

When Koz came to head up the C-17 project, things changed rapidly. He saw that the plane was being built as usual, one section at a time, and knew there was a better way. He also saw that quality needed a big boost and began a campaign focused on quality, schedule, and cost. One day Koz announced that the plane would not move until it was complete because quality was job one. He totally believed that schedule and cost would follow if his people would focus on quality. While most people thought his vision was crazy, he stayed the course and kept driving home his quality speech. Things started to change for the better. Because Koz had built such credibility with his people, they didn't want to be the reason the plane wasn't moving. They broke through many of the old barriers to build the plane, getting assistance from leadership when necessary. This resulted in higher-quality planes that were delivered early to their customers.

(Summarized from *The Heart of Change,* pages 73–76)

- A common mantra is "quality, schedule, cost—in that order." Have you sometimes begun implementation before the product was "complete in position"? What was the impact of your decisions?

- Do you look for creative ways to achieve your objectives and still hold to quality, schedule, and cost, in that order?

- Has your leadership earned the respect and credibility to successfully launch a bold vision?

"The Body in the Living Room"

As Ron Marshall contemplated the speed at which the organization should undergo change, he thought back to a story his realtor told him—when you move into a new house, you need to have a plan for fixing it up in the first six months; after that you don't see the bodies in the middle of the living room. What was once unacceptable becomes acceptable. In addition, slower change often instills added fear. Recognizing that slow change may be acceptable under certain circumstances, Ron's organization nevertheless decided to move fast.

(Summarized from *The Heart of Change,* pages 78–79)

- What bodies do you have in your living room?

- What needs to be done to remove the bodies?

- What barriers are in the way and how will you overcome them?

More Resources

Abrahams, Jeffrey. **Mission Statement Book: 301 Corporate Mission Statements from America's Top Companies**. Berkeley, CA: Ten Speed Press, 1999.

Recognizing that organizations can learn from many of America's top companies, Abrahams compiled a collection of more than three hundred mission statements to help companies translate their strategic vision into a solid mission statement. Using examples such as Federal Express and General Motors along with practical and comprehensive advice, this book will help any organization develop an effective mission statement.

Belasco, James A., and Stead, Jerre. **Soaring with the Phoenix: Renewing the Vision, Reviving the Spirit, and Re-Creating the Success of Your Company.** New York: Warren Books, 1999.

Belasco and Stead share their "revolutionary" approach to methodically reenergizing employees. This includes placing a renewed emphasis on learning, establishing a performance-driven culture emphasizing accountability, building stronger customer and partner relationships to not only meet but exceed expectations, and strengthening the focus on the customer.

Collins, James C. **Good to Great: Why Some Companies Make the Leap . . . and Others Don't**. New York: HarperCollins Publishers, 2001.

Collins presents many startling and counterintuitive insights into what enables certain organizations to make the transformation from good to great. He explores what it really takes to achieve an organization's vision of being great.

Collins, James C., and Porras, Jerry I. "Building Your Company's Vision." **Harvard Business Review**, Sept. 1996.

In this **HBR** article, Collins and Porras offer a new, clear, and rigorous framework for vision creation. They explain why it is essential to link vision statements to the core purpose and values of an organization while allowing the strategies and practices of a company to endlessly adapt to a changing world.

Goodstein, Leonard David, Nolan, Timothy, and J. William Pfeiffer **Applied Strategic Planning: How to Develop a Plan That Really Works**. New York: McGraw-Hill, 1993.

These three successful strategic planning consultants compiled their experiences working with top companies across the country to create a practical guide to developing and implementing long-term competitive strategies. By emphasizing key business drivers and organizational levers, this book is superior to many other strategic planning manuals because it gets to the heart of how organizations can integrate strategic direction into everyday operations.

Kim, W. Chan, and Mauborgne, Renée A. "Charting Your Company's Future." **Harvard Business Review**, June 2002.

Creating a clear, strategic vision is a difficult challenge for most companies. Rather than getting lost in data and conflicting agendas, companies should start with a picture, a "strategy canvas," from which all leaders can continue the strategy development process in alignment.

Schwartz, Peter. **The Art of the Long View: Planning for the Future in an Uncertain World**. New York: Doubleday, 1996.

This revolutionary guide to future planning describes a powerful tool for developing strategic vision and applying the intuitive skills used by artists and musicians to navigate the future.

Weisbord, Marvin R., and Janoff, Sandra. **Future Search: An Action Guide to Finding Common Ground in Organizations and Communities**. New York: Berrett-Koehler Publishers, 1999.

This book explains what a 'future state search conference' is, how one is conducted and where people with a stake in the organization's future gather to generate creative strategies.

PART II

Engaging and Enabling the Whole Organization

ONCE YOU HAVE ESTABLISHED A CLIMATE for change, you can begin to think about how you will engage and enable the organization. This is the focus of the next three steps: communicate for buy-in, enable action, and create short-term wins.

A common misconception in organizational transformation is that training will be enough to ready employees for their job changes. While training does help prepare individuals for the technical aspects of their jobs, it often does not encompass everything needed to sustain long-term success. When individuals begin training without any understanding of the changes and their specific impacts, they spend much of their time coming to grips with how their job is changing and how they will be affected. When resistance, in the form of fear, anger, or complacency, is in the way, true learning cannot occur.

Preparing and executing an event-driven communication plan that establishes two-way dialogue with stakeholders can help set realistic expectations and eliminate resistance that threatens the transformation. To enable employees to take action, it is important to redesign or update HR-related processes (e.g., performance metrics and appraisals, organization structure, rewards, succession planning) as well as redefine roles and responsibilities in a way that reinforces new behaviors. In other words, people at all levels need to understand their responsibilities, and leaders need to be consistent in holding them accountable, evaluating their performance, and rewarding them. Achieving and communicating short-term wins demonstrates to the organization that the change is gaining momentum and is here to stay.

As you read the next three chapters, I encourage you to think about the techniques that have worked to engage and enable your organization in past transformation efforts. What characteristics made those techniques successful? What techniques did not work?

Communicate for Buy-In

In successful change efforts, the vision and strategies are not locked in a room with the guiding team. The direction of change is widely communicated, and communicated for both understanding and gut-level buy-in. The goal: to get as many people as possible acting to make the vision a reality.

Vision communication fails for many reasons. Perhaps the most obvious is lack of clarity. People wonder: "What are they talking about?" Usually, this lack of clarity means step 3 has been done poorly. Fussy or illogical visions and strategies cannot be communicated with clarity and sound logic. But, in addition, step 4 has its own set of distinct challenges that can undermine a transformation, even if the vision is perfect.

—from Step 4 of *The Heart of Change*

Purpose

Developing and creating the *right* vision for change is obviously crucial to transformational success. But effectively communicating the vision and how it will be achieved is the key to capturing the commitment of the workforce. If leadership has taken the time to craft candid, concise, and heartfelt messages, employees will grasp the possibilities of the vision and get on board. However, if the workforce does not see the alignment of word and deed, they will simply write off the change effort as another "strategy du jour" and continue work as usual.

Approach

Communication is more than merely a discrete step in the change process. Rather, it is an ever-continuing effort to convey key messages that shift over time as awareness of the change effort increases and individuals commit to the vision. If you are seeking to raise urgency as well as build guiding teams, communicating with key individuals and groups is obviously critical to these efforts and should have already taken place. Organizational change, by definition, cannot take place in a vacuum; communicating in a concise, candid, heartfelt manner is critical to the success of your change effort.

Helping individuals progress from total lack of awareness of the problem to understanding and committing to the vision as noted in step 3, typically includes the following key activities:

1. Initially communicating the vision.

2. Engaging in continuous dialogue with the stakeholders.

3. Enrolling stakeholders in the change effort.

Figure 4-1 illustrates how these activities map to the three key phases for achieving organizational transformation.

Initially, persuasively communicating the vision will help create awareness of the problem and open people to the possibility of a new future for the organization. Mobilizing commitment to a vision, however, requires much more than the simple communication of a desirable future. Full collaboration and support for the vision is

FIGURE 4-1

Approach to building commitment

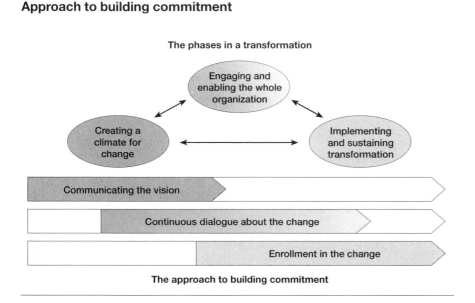

achieved mainly through continuous dialogue, stakeholder enroll-ment, clear accountability for results, and ongoing attention to the change effort. To paraphrase John F. Kennedy, things do not just happen; they are made to happen.

Communicating the Vision

The objective of communication in a change effort is to influence people to think and act in accordance with a new direction. To fully realize the vision, the communication needs to reach everyone in the organization who will play a role in making it a reality. Table 4-1 offers suggestions and tactics for how to communicate the vision effectively.

A critical aspect of the communication effort is getting feedback about the level of understanding and acceptance of the vision. To achieve this:

TABLE 4-1

Tactics to guide effective communication of the vision

Develop a compelling story

- Provide a context for the change.
- Focus on why, why now, what, and how.
- Develop high-level messages that capture the gist of the comprehensive vision.

Keep it simple

- Use short statements.
- Avoid jargon specific to a profession.

Use metaphors and analogies

- Use images to depict the future state of the organization.
- Use an analogy to explain the different phases in the process of change.

Repeat, repeat, repeat

- Use every opportunity to link day-to-day business activities and decisions with the vision.
- Continue to reinforce the messages throughout the entire change process.

Use many different forums to spread the message

- Make it a habit to refer to elements of the vision in every communication, formal and informal.
- Have all levels of the organization seek ways to repeat and reinforce the key messages.

Make it multidirectional

- The vision will live through the interactions with people. Encourage as many people as possible to talk about it—peer to peer, front-line managers to staff, staff to customers, etc.

Build linkages to initiatives

- Explain how all the change initiatives contribute to the achievement of the vision.

Align leadership actions to communications

- Ensure that leadership actions and decisions are consistent with the new direction.
- Explicitly address all inconsistencies.
- Shape and reinforce existing congruent behaviors.
- Have the guiding teams model the expected behaviors.

Integrate communication initiatives

- Build a common set of key messages that can be integrated into all communications.

Source: Adapted from John P. Kotter, *Leading Change* (Boston: Harvard Business School Press, 1996); John P. Kotter and Dan S. Cohen, *The Heart of Change: Real-Life Stories of How People Change Their Organizations* (Boston: Harvard Business School Press, 2002).

- Consider the use of focus groups, evaluations, and debriefs to collect feedback.

- Test understanding by asking people to describe what the vision means for them and how it affects them.

- Seek feedback and questions.

- Follow up on the feedback received.

- Listen, listen, listen.

Engaging in Continuous Dialogue with Stakeholders

Throughout the change process, the guiding teams need continuous dialogue with all stakeholders. The objective of this dialogue is to detect resistance and use it to advantage, as well as build commitment by:

- Obtaining feedback from stakeholders as the change develops.

- Preparing stakeholders to absorb the change.

Maintaining this dialogue can be a daunting task for the guiding team because the communication often:

- Targets many people with different needs.

- Is multidirectional.

- Involves many kinds of information in different formats.

- Involves multiple types of information technology.

Enrolling the Organization in the Change Effort

Communication improves the quality of decisions and the strength of commitment to those decisions. The process of creating commitment is not achieved in one step, but with the gradual involvement of stakeholders in the change. As change progresses, stakeholders must be "enrolled" in the change; that is, they must develop increasing levels of understanding and commitment to the effort as they are called upon to take action. For this enrollment to take place, communication must be clear, continual, and constantly responsive to the perspectives of the stakeholders. Table 4-2 depicts the appropriate enrollment strategy for each stage in the process.

Managing stakeholder enrollment is complex for several reasons:

- Different groups need to be involved in varying degrees at different stages of the change.

- Different groups have different communication needs.

- Not everybody needs or wants to move along the continuum at the same speed.

Assessment tool 4-1 offers an example of a stakeholder enrollment map. In this tool, each key stakeholder group is identified and then assessed as to its current level of enrollment as well as the desired level of enrollment. Where a gap exists (between the current and desired state), a plan must be developed to move the stakeholder group to the desired level of enrollment.

TABLE 4-2

Engaging the stakeholders: the enrollment process

	Awareness	**Understanding**	**Collaboration**	**Commitment**	**Advocacy**
Definition	Stakeholders are aware of and understand change purpose and progress	Stakeholders have a sound understanding of the benefits and implications of the change for them	Stakeholders support the change, believe it is worthwhile, and would act if prompted	Stakeholders proactively communicate and take action required in support of the change	Stakeholders take initiatives to improve and sustain the performance
Strategy	Kept informed	Participating in project	Given meaningful roles	Given accountabilities	Given ownership

ASSESSMENT TOOL 4-1

Example of format for stakeholder enrollment plan

Stakeholder group	Unaware	Aware	Understand	Collaborate	Commit	Advocate
Business units					◉	○
Geographic units			◉		○	
Functional units		◉		○		
Employees and customers		◉		○		
Other stakeholders	◉	○				

◉ Current   ○ Desired

Before executing these three key activities, consider the following tools, questions, and advice to help you communicate more clearly and effectively.

Communication Planning Tools

The most formidable challenge in continuous communication is dealing with the complexity and magnitude of this task, given the size of the audience and the amount of information to circulate. The following four tools may help in the process:

- A template for assessing audiences.

- A matrix for prioritizing audiences.

- A set of questions for defining the communication process.

- A map for aligning communications with the change process.

The Audience Assessment Template and the Audience Prioritization Matrix

To bring the entire organization on board, you need to think about all stakeholders as audiences whose needs you must fully understand if your message is to be effective. The Audience Assessment Template (assessment tool 4-2) and the Audience Prioritization Matrix (assessment tool 4-3) are designed to identify all internal and external stakeholders, assess their needs, and prioritize the audiences for communication. The template provides a simple framework for considering and recording the needs of each key group or individual, understanding how the change affects them, and predicting concerns and/or issues each group may have. In addition, it provides a focus for communicating with each audience about their critical role in the success of the initiative, the level of effort required of them, and the degree of commitment to the change they must have.

Once the Audience Assessment Template is completed, stakeholders and stakeholder groups can be plotted on the Audience Prioritization Matrix and thus help focus the communication planning effort. Stakeholders should be plotted individually on the matrix, although those stakeholders that fall into the same quadrant may be grouped together and defined as one audience. In some situations, however, you may have multiple audiences within a quadrant. The "Maintain Confidence" and "Woo and Win" audiences are most critical to the project's success and thus require the greatest level of effort. The "Keep Informed" audience requires the next greatest level of effort, followed by the "Monitor and Respond" audience.

Questions for Defining the Communication Process

A few key questions in the following areas can help define and simplify the communication process.

- *The audience:* The challenge is to maintain a dialogue with multiple stakeholders who may have different needs at different times. The following questions help to target groups:

    ✓ Which stakeholders are impacted by the change?

    ✓ What information do they need?

- *The cascading process:* Communication is most effective not only when it is timely and appropriate, but also when the

Audience assessment template

Stakeholder or group	Description of stakeholder or groups	Criticality to success (1–5)	How the change affects this audience	Effort required to change (1–5)	Concerns/issues (what this audience needs)	Degree of commitment (– 0 +)

1 = low; 5 = high

ASSESSMENT TOOL 4-3

Audience prioritization matrix

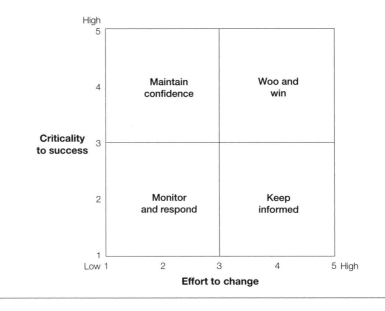

messenger is a person close to the stakeholders, such as their manager. A cascading approach in which leaders in each successive level communicate to the next lower level, allows information to be delivered in terms that are meaningful, as well as set in the right context by a trusted person.

✓ Who will deliver the information to each stakeholder group?

✓ Whom will the stakeholders trust with this information?

✓ What will be the source of that information?

✓ What tone and message do you want to communicate?

• *The feedback process:* There must always be a feedback loop. The challenge is to maintain open communication channels at all times with the stakeholders.

✓ What feedback is needed and from whom?

✓ How will it be collected?

✓ What channels can the stakeholders use to ask questions and raise issues?

✓ How can confidentiality be established and maintained?

- *The follow-through process:* The challenge is not only to receive feedback, but also to respond to it. What mechanism will be used to ensure that someone will:

    ✓ Take action on issues?

    ✓ Capture and act on good ideas?

    ✓ Clarify uncertainty and answer questions?

    ✓ Thank people for their communication?

A Map for Aligning Communications with the Change Process

Communications should reflect the different realities within the organization as the change initiative progresses and individuals react to the outcomes. Table 4-4 offers a "map" that aligns the various steps of the change process with appropriate communication responses.

Guidelines for Orchestrating Effective Dialogue

Defining the Communication Process

Once the audiences are defined, the Communication Plan Template (assessment tool 4-3) can help focus and simplify the communication process for each stakeholder group. This template will help answer questions like these:

- What information needs does the audience have?

- What is the desired response?

- What is the likely response?

- How will the information be communicated into the organization?

- How should the message be delivered (via what channel)? How often?

TABLE 4-2

Communicating the right message at the right time

Step in the change process	Typical reactions in the organization	Appropriate communication responses and emphasis
Guiding team members are recruited. Vision is developed. Change effort is still small. (Steps 1, 2)	• Individuals are unaware of the need for change.	• Communication creates broad awareness of the change and support from early adopters. • Communication emphasizes the need for change and bring awareness and dissatisfaction with "what is." • Leaders actively demonstrate support.
Vision is developed and communicated. Early adopters get involved in the change. (Steps 3, 4)	• Individuals are curious about the change. • Pessimism about likely success is frequently apparent.	• Both broad and targeted communications educate stakeholders about the future and the change that will happen. • Communication gets a critical mass of stakeholders to understand the change. • Leaders continue reinforcing the need for change. • Two-way channels are open: Leaders are listening and learning what meaning the vision has for people and adjusting their message as required.
Major decisions with high impact are made. Initial changes are visible. (Steps 5, 6)	• Anxiety about potential loss. • Avoidance.	• Communication gets critical mass to collaborate in the change. • Two-way dialogue takes place on the details of the change. • Sacrifices are acknowledged but communication continues to reinforce the need for change. • High urgency levels are maintained.
Major changes are implemented. (Step 7)	• Chaos. • Stress.	• Supportive "survival" communication clarifies expectations and resources available and provides guidance. • Boundaries are clarified—what is changing and what is not. • Pain is acknowledged but the need for change is continually reinforced. • Visible short-term wins are created.
Postchange. Effort level reduced. (Step 8)	• Fatigue.	• Successes are celebrated but the need for change is continually emphasized.

Communication plan template

Communication/ action	Key messages/ details	Audience targeted	Due date	Channel	Responsibility			Status
					Develop	Review/approve	Deliver	

- Who should deliver the message?

- How will we capture their feedback and input?

- How will we follow through on their feedback and input?

- How will we measure communication effectiveness?

The template is designed to help identify the messages that need to be communicated to various audiences. Once drafted, the communication plan can be sorted to help you determine if all audiences are included, if a variety of solid communication channels are targeted, and if the proposed timing will work with the change timeline. It is important to view any such template as a "living document" that is constantly reviewed and updated.

Adapting Communication During the Change Process

Typically, as the change initiative progresses, its pace increases and anxiety rises in the organization. The communication effort must keep up with and reflect the ever-shifting realities within the organization. For example, individuals will start at different levels of commitment and continue at different levels. Some will be active supporters, some will resist the change, and the rest may be waiting to see what happens before they make a judgment. Therefore, the main thrust of the communication effort must be three-pronged:

- Create a critical mass of supporters for the change as fast as possible.

- Maintain the commitment of supporters.

Seek out and "work" the resisters; that is, keep tabs on their views and needs, respond with persuasive arguments for change, and help them to see and feel its rationale.

Understanding Resistance

Resistance is a normal and expected emotional reaction to change. Experienced, effective leaders know this, and also understand that resistance can be turned into a positive factor for several reasons:

- Resistance indicates that the pressure for change is being felt.

- It is a source of feedback for modifying and refining the vision and the change plan.

- It highlights where the vision is being tested against real conditions.

- It is a potential source of information to improve the vision or the change plan, as well as an opportunity to engage a group of employees in the change process.

There are really two main types of resistance: "logical" resistance, which comes from philosophical differences with the vision and rationale, or genuine differences on how to go about effecting the needed change; and "emotional" resistance, which is really just a knee-jerk, reflexive reaction against changing familiar ways of doing things. Logical resistance can be both the toughest to deal with and the most useful in gauging how you shape and communicate your vision. Emotional resistance is most common and has the greatest potential for being converted into support and motivation.

Make sure you always stay well attuned to the levels of change resistance, where it is coming from and why, and how it changes over time. Leaders who neglect to be sensitive to resistance in these ways are often blindsided by it later on, when they think all is going smoothly.

Outcomes

You know your communication efforts have achieved critical buy-in when you see these signs of acceptance:

- A shared understanding of the business vision and the strategic plan to achieve that vision.

- A shared picture of a desirable future, which is necessary to motivate people and coordinate the kinds of actions that spark transformations.

- An appreciation of the rationale for the change, which enables stakeholders to see and feel the need for change and become committed to the new direction.

- Minimized resistance to change.

- Sufficient belief in the change effort and trust in the change agents for individuals to commit to the change.

Key Implementation Challenges

Keeping communication channels open and effective during a change initiative can be challenging on two primary fronts. You must determine the right amount of information to convey in terms of both frequency and volume. In addition, it is critical that leaders "walk the talk" if the communication effort is to be credible.

Avoid Information Overload

While the vision and the status of the change effort should be communicated often, be careful that the message is not lost in over-used channels of communication. Unclogging channels or creating new or alternative channels will emphasize the message and make it stand out among the countless other pieces of information employees receive. If you have not used Web sites before, set one up. When leaders are out talking to the workforce and updating them on organizational matters, be sure that they have one or two points to discuss about the vision and that you update the points on a regular basis. See if you can get key points about the vision included in various staff meetings. Look for other channels that are not customarily utilized for this type of communication.

Sending Consistent Messages

By now, the urgency level is high, teams have been formed and/or are in the process of being formed, the vision has been created, and communicating the vision is under way. However, if the actions of a highly visible leader or member of one of the teams contradict the vision, this can send a message to the rest of the organization that speaks louder than any memo, e-mail, or newsletter. The message says that the organization is not completely serious about the change and not all leaders support it. For instance, what is the effect when leaders call for cost containment but continue to spend as usual? What do people think when a manager asks everybody, for greater efficiency, to input their own time/expense data electronically—but continues to have his assistant complete his own form? Leaders must be extra attentive to appearances during any significant change effort—people are watching, even more than usual.

Gauging Effectiveness

Key Indicators of Effective Communication

You'll know that the key messages embedded in the vision have been effectively communicated to the organization when you see some of the following behaviors:

- Managers can concisely express the vision in their own words.

- Managers can articulate what the change means for their unit or group.

- There are discussions about the vision, the goals, and the strategy in routine management meetings, and in formal and informal gatherings.

- The vision works its way into everyday memos, presentations, and company communications to employees, customers, and shareholders.

- More questions about the change initiative are addressed to the managers, leaders, guiding teams, and others participating in the change.

- Terms used in the vision start to become part of the language used throughout the organization.

In particular, in management meetings, you'll begin to see these behaviors:

- Managers use every opportunity to bring the vision into conversation to support routine decisions and actions.

- Managers behave in a manner that is consistent with the vision.

- Managers intelligently question the different impacts the vision may have on their plans.

In the organization in general, more support for the change is in evidence:

- Employees have more excitement, energy, and focus to tackle problems because they have clear guidance and goals.

- More individuals come forward voluntarily to offer their assistance and support.

- Decisions are made that break from past ways of thinking and acting and are consistent with the new vision.

- Employees express dissatisfaction about the current work environment.

Equally important, you'll know that communication efforts are having impact when more resistance to the change emerges:

- The vision (or its communicators) may be contested, argued, or criticized.

- Numerous guiding teams and leaders of the organization get push-back from various parts of the organization about the validity of the vision or the feasibility of the strategy.

- Complaints surface that the vision is too much of a departure from the "way we do things."

The Communication Diagnostic

Communicating the vision is the key to building the organization's commitment to the new vision. It also effectively sets the stage for making the change a reality. This tool will help determine the effectiveness of your communication efforts and should be used multiple times throughout the change initiative.

To use the diagnostic successfully, follow these steps:

- Distribute the Communication Diagnostic (assessment tool 4-5) to the individuals whose perspective is desired.

- Ask the individuals being surveyed to answer the questions according to their own experiences and knowledge of the organization.

- As indicated on the directions that accompany the diagnostic, respondents will assign a rating of 1 to 6 to each question, with 1 indicating "strongly disagree" and 6 indicating "strongly agree."

- Tally the results after the sheets have been returned to you. The farther the results are from the maximum score possible, the more pressing the problem.

Suggestions for Improvement

Low scores on this questionnaire could be due to many factors. Perhaps you're sending out the appropriate information, but it is getting lost

ASSESSMENT TOOL 4-5

The communication diagnostic

Instructions

- Please read each statement and indicate the extent to which it describes the norm in your organization as a whole. Your responses should reflect what you have experienced as well as what you have generally observed in your organization.
- Answer the questions using a 6-point scale; the far left of the scale indicates that you strongly disagree and the far right of the scale indicates that you strongly agree. Please respond by checking the box that corresponds most closely to your situation.
- If you do not know the answer, check the "Do not know" box.
- Please take the time to respond to the open-ended questions at the end of the survey. Your responses are crucial in improving the change initiative.
- Be honest in your responses. There are no right or wrong answers, and your answers will remain completely confidential.

Communication	Strongly disagree (1)				Strongly agree (6)		Do not know
As a member of this organization, I . . .							
1. Feel that the change initiative is communicated effectively, giving everyone a solid understanding of our future.	☐	☐	☐	☐	☐	☐	☐
2. Feel that the change initiative has been explained in clear terms.	☐	☐	☐	☐	☐	☐	☐
3. Feel that the change initiative is communicated frequently.	☐	☐	☐	☐	☐	☐	☐
4. Feel informed on the progress of the initiative.	☐	☐	☐	☐	☐	☐	☐
5. Do not feel overloaded with data, because communications have been clear and heartfelt.	☐	☐	☐	☐	☐	☐	☐
6. See multiple forms of communication (e.g., large and small meetings, one-to-one discussions, memos, newsletters, e-mails, conference calls, etc.) being used to communicate the change initiative.	☐	☐	☐	☐	☐	☐	☐
7. See leadership avidly communicating the need for change and why it is in our best interests.	☐	☐	☐	☐	☐	☐	☐
8. See managers avidly communicating the need for change and why it is in our best interests.	☐	☐	☐	☐	☐	☐	☐
9. See that leadership doesn't just talk about the change vision, but leads by example.	☐	☐	☐	☐	☐	☐	☐
10. See that managers don't just talk about the change vision, but lead by example.	☐	☐	☐	☐	☐	☐	☐
11. Feel that activities in our organization that are inconsistent with our change vision have been clearly explained.	☐	☐	☐	☐	☐	☐	☐
12. Receive clear (not mixed) signals about the change initiative.	☐	☐	☐	☐	☐	☐	☐

(continued)

ASSESSMENT TOOL 4-5

The communication diagnostic *(continued)*

Communication	Strongly disagree (1)					Strongly agree (6)	Do not know
13. See that feedback mechanisms for employees to express their opinions and interests in the change initiative are in place.	☐	☐	☐	☐	☐	☐	☐
14. Believe that those feedback mechanisms are being used.	☐	☐	☐	☐	☐	☐	☐
15. Feel that there is a constant dialogue between all levels of the organization regarding the change initiative.	☐	☐	☐	☐	☐	☐	☐
Subtotals	x 1	+ x 2	+ x 3	+ x 4	+ x 5	+ x 6	
= Grand total							

To get your totals

Add the check marks in vertical columns to get subtotals. Multiply that total by the number at the bottom of each column. Then add the subtotals together to get the grand total.

Grand total: 15 = serious problems, 90 = no problems. Any score below a 60 indicates a need for improvement.

Open-ended feedback

1. What communication activities have been most successful thus far? What made them successful?

_____
_____
_____
_____
_____

2. What communication activities have been least successful thus far? What didn't you like about the communication?

_____
_____
_____
_____
_____

3. Are there any specific communications that you would like to see ended?

_____
_____
_____
_____
_____

4. Are there any specific communications that you would like to see started?

_____
_____
_____
_____
_____

The communication diagnostic *(continued)*

5. Without referring to outside aids, write your organization's vision statement, to the best of your knowledge, in the space provided below.

_____

_____

_____

_____

_____

6. Through what types of communication have you received information about the vision?

_____

_____

_____

_____

_____

amid countless other memos or newsletters. Maybe you are using the right channel, but your message is too complicated and long-winded to keep anyone's attention. Maybe your managers' and executives' actions are not consistent with the vision, thus sending mixed messages. Or, perhaps you do not have a clear understanding of your stakeholders' needs and anxieties, and thus you're not certain why they are resisting change. Regardless of the reason, in any change initiative, effective communication is key to driving the process forward and overcoming resistance. Any of these factors could lead to the unraveling of much thinking, planning, and hard work. The following suggestions may help improve your communication efforts.

Focus Communications

Your desire to communicate the vision, the rationale for change, and recent developments in the change process does not mean you should bombard members of the organization with endless information. Many common channels of communication are already overused, crammed with junk, and thus largely ignored by employees. In addition, communicators often use multiple channels simultaneously to ensure that the point is understood. Remember, quantity is not quality. To keep your communications focused, try developing a new channel for communication. This can be a creative process, and the newness of the communication vehicle encourages recipients to notice and remember the information. Another strategy is to purge the existing channels so they are not so crammed with unnecessary communications.

Prioritize the Messages You Want to Communicate

Decide which messages are most important for your employees to know. For instance, if many people cannot accurately paraphrase the vision statement or describe the behaviors needed to achieve the vision, you are not communicating clearly. In any change initiative, it is vital that everyone understand the vision that they are working toward and the behaviors that support or work against it.

Simplify Communication

Often, we send messages that are too complicated or long-winded, and the audience quickly loses interest or becomes confused. Effective communication should speak to the audience, not just in the professional and business sense, but through the heart and the head as well. Avoid technical talk and business acronyms when possible. Steer clear of complicated numbers and figures. Address concerns and anxieties about the change initiative and be honest about what you do and do not know.

Use Other Forms of Communication

Keep in mind that communication is not confined to words. As the saying goes, "actions speak louder than words." The actions of executives and leaders make a strong impression on everyone in the organization. If their behaviors or actions do not correspond to the change initiative and the vision, others will notice. Symbols are also a good way to illustrate the vision. For instance, creating an emblem that symbolizes the essence of the vision helps people identify with the vision. In a complementary way, be sure to remove or modify aspects of the work environment that do not match the vision message.

Ensure That Your Communication Plan Is Two-Way

The Communication Diagnostic provides an excellent feedback mechanism for employees to express opinions about the change. Ensure that communication channels stay open in all directions— upward, downward, and sideways. This increases the probability that potential difficulties can be recognized and rectified early in the process.

Checkpoint: Move Forward or Revisit Prior Steps?

How are you doing? Here are a few warning signs that you may have to revisit some prior steps in the change process before moving forward:

- If the vision seems understood but there is no evidence that it influences decisions or behavior, then the need for change is not shared and accepted. This could indicate that urgency is low, there is a lack of alignment among the guiding teams, or the vision needs more clarification.

- If the communication efforts generate no feedback (positive or negative), the vision may not be clearly understood, or it may not be getting through. In this case, you should revisit the vision to ensure that it is "right," that is, clearly responsive to the relevant organizational situation or context. If your message is not being heard, you may want to get feedback on the effectiveness and quality of your communications regarding the change effort.

Stories to Remember from Step 4 of *The Heart of Change*

Use the following story summaries and questions to help you develop and execute your communication plan.

"Preparing for Q and A"

As this organization sought to transition to a team-based environment, twenty managers were assigned to the communication team. This team, which eventually spoke with every worker and trade union, spent a great deal of time planning not only their presentation, but also their responses to the questions they would receive. To prepare for the Q and A, they used role playing, in which a mock audience attempted to critique and poke holes in the presentation. This exercise resulted in a support document containing clear, simple, and concise answers to two hundred questions. With a lot of practice, the twenty communicators became comfortable with new information and techniques for responding to the audience and were successful in their communication campaign as a result.   (Summarized from *The Heart of Change*, pages 84–86)

- How are leaders preparing to communicate with their constituents? Will they be seen as credible? How will they create faith in the change effort?

- How will they answer the really tough questions? Have they got their "story" together?

"My Portal"

Fred Woods, responsible for communication in his organization, believed that communication channels were clogged or ineffective. He felt that managers needed to be the primary communicator; however, the communications group could help clear the channels. After looking into the problem further, Fred's team found that 80 percent of messages were neither wanted nor needed by employees. To solve the problem, Fred's team began working on a portal concept so each employee could customize the type of information received.

(Summarized from *The Heart of Change,* pages 89–91)

- Do your communication processes create the desire for information from employees?

- What do people want to learn about the change effort?

- How much information clutter exists and what can be done to reduce it?

- How can you better utilize technology to get your message out?

"Nuking the Executive Floor"

While the company's vision was to be a low-cost producer, the employees wondered how that was possible given the extravagant amenities and furnishings on the executive floor. Over the years, there was discussion about remodeling, but leadership always had an excuse for not being able to do it. When a new CEO entered the picture, he immediately had the executive floor remodeled to reflect more modest values, in line with the company's history. Employees felt more comfortable visiting the executive floor, and they believed that their leaders were walking the talk.   (Summarized from *The Heart of Change,* pages 92–94)

- Are the actions of your leaders drowning out their words?

- How can members of the guiding teams help each other examine their behavior to ensure it is aligned with the vision?

- What actions do you take when you find inconsistencies between word and deed?

"The Screen Saver"

As employees turned on their computers one morning, for the first time they all had the same screen saver: "We will be #1 in the U.K. market by 2001." While this new vision had already been communicated to employees, leadership wanted a way to continually reinforce the message so employees would know that this was a serious goal. The screen saver got people talking, and departments started setting goals that would help the company achieve the vision. Although there were skeptics who did not want to change, many people began believing the vision was attainable. Periodically, the message was changed and metrics were added to the screen saver, and over time, the image became an icon that helped people stay focused on goals.

(Summarized from *The Heart of Change,* pages 95–97)

- How can you utilize technology more creatively?

- How can you surprise your organization into a new way of seeing?

- What are some simple, candid, and heartfelt ways to update people regarding the change effort?

More Resources

D'Aprix, Roger. **Communicating for Change: Connecting the Workplace with the Marketplace**. San Francisco: Jossey-Bass, 1996.

> Communication is never more critical than during times of change. D'Aprix discusses common communication breakdowns, and his strategic communication model demonstrates how to align communication at all levels to help employees understand and commit to changes.

Hirschhorn, Larry. "Campaigning for Change." **Harvard Business Review**, July 2002.

> The most important aspect of change is execution. Hirschhorn describes the three types of campaigns—political, marketing, and military—required to make a transformation program successful.

Larkin, T. J., and Larkin, Sandar. **Communicating Change: How to Win Employee Support for New Business Goals**. New York: McGraw-Hill, 1994.

Successful change requires effective communication in order to enlist the support and cooperation of employees. This work provides numerous tools and resources for planning, creating, and evaluating change communication.

Mai, Robert, and Akerson, Alan. **The Leader as Communicator: Strategies and Tactics to Build Loyalty, Focus Effort, and Spark Creativity**. New York: AMACOM, 2003.

Three challenges are universal for leaders trying to keep their company at the top of the industry, build a sense of community, keep employees focused through even the toughest transitions, and spark creativity. Communication is the most crucial competency leaders need in order to overcome these challenges. The authors examine the communication-based roles a leader must master and present case studies from top organizations.

Saunders, Rebecca. "Communicating Change: A Dozen Tips from the Experts." **Harvard Management Communication Letter**, Aug. 1999.

Even the most positive change can leave employees resentful and confused when communication is not effective. Saunders outlines twelve tips from experts to prevent morale problems and make change initiatives successful.

Stauffer, David. "How to Win the Buy-in: Setting the Stage for Change." **Harvard Management Update**, June 2003.

This article presents findings from three different change initiatives at different companies. Successful approaches include (1) Tell it like it is; (2) break the initiative into manageable chunks; (3) hear employees out; and (4) rely on bottom-up and top-down techniques. Using these ideas, your change initiative might actually get implemented instead of ignored.

Enable Action

In highly successful change efforts, when people begin to understand and act on a change vision, you remove barriers in their paths. You take away the tattered sails and give them better ones. You take a wind in their faces and create a wind at their backs. You take away a pessimistic skipper and give the crew an optimistic boss.

—from Step 5 of *The Heart of Change*

Purpose

By creating a clear, compelling vision, you've given employees a reason to change. But now, if you want them to carry out that vision, you have to provide them with not only the motive but also the means to do so. The purpose of this step is to enable a broad base of people to take action by removing as many barriers to the implementation of the change vision as possible. Those who have read *The Heart of Change* or *Leading Change* will note that this step has been renamed. It is now called "enable action" rather than "empower action." The reason is simple—in talking with a few thousand readers I was told that "busting barriers" is much more about enabling than it is about empowering. In addition, I heard over and over again

·

that the word *empower* has connotations that carry a great deal of excess baggage, and the way John Kotter and I talk about this step, *enable* sets the right picture.

Approach

Enabling a broad base of employees to take action involves two simple things:

1. Busting barriers that block people from carrying out the vision.

2. Encouraging people to take risks and be innovative.

Busting Barriers

The four main barriers that often need busting are organizational structure, lack of skills, organizational systems, and resistant leaders and managers. Below are brief descriptions of each obstacle, as well as strategies to overcome them.

Structure
Organizational structure can often fragment the change effort and stymie progress as well as communication. You run into this obstacle when change initiatives require people from multiple areas to work together, but the needed resources and authority are fragmented throughout the organization. Other structural barriers may exist:

- Functional silos drive different focuses and priorities, quickly stalling any progress.

- Individual silos within functional silos don't communicate with each other.

- People are told they can act on their own only to find that their decisions must go through middle managers who don't want to relinquish control of decision making.

Here are some quick tips and strategies for removing the structural obstacles that make it difficult for people to take action:

- Align authority with responsibility. Ensure that position descriptions accurately reflect the power to accomplish the tasks for which people are held accountable. Regroup necessary resources. Ensure that the reporting structure is properly aligned with the strategy.

- Clarify priorities for people who report to multiple groups. Take the time to resolve competing priorities/initiatives.

- Reduce interference from other groups by isolating the group driving the change initiative if necessary. Make it clear to other groups in the organization what the key priorities are and how they will be measured and monitored.

- Create a structure for the initiative that is consistent with the vision. The vision should drive responsibilities, resources, and information toward the goals.

Skills

When the environment changes, your organization needs to change with it, and that means people's skills need to change, too. The new environment often requires knowledge, skills, abilities, and attitudes that are different from those needed in the past. A lack of necessary skills can slow or even stall needed action. What's more, habits built over years may have lost their relevance in the new context, but nevertheless are very hard to break.

Here are some suggestions for addressing a skills gap:

- Explicitly define the new behaviors and identify the knowledge, skills, abilities, and attitudes that will be needed to succeed in the new working environment:

- Visit other sites or companies where these skills and abilities are being employed.

- Ask the people who will be doing the new work what skills they have and what training they will need to be successful.

- Test how the new skills will work in a pilot setting.

- Provide training to develop the new skills and attitudes:

  ✓ *At the right time:* Training should not only help people to start in their new roles but also provide follow-up to help solve problems related to the change later on.

  ✓ *For the right skills:* People are often taught the technical skills but not the social skills to make the transition. Be sure individuals have the change leadership skills to accept and perform well in the new environment.

  ✓ *Using the right approach:* An educational experience where a real-life scenario is acted out may be more effective than a lecture. Clearly, do not rely solely on eLearning, as this will send the wrong message.

Systems

Related to structure, specific organizational systems and processes, such as compensation, performance management, training, talent management, and so on, often perpetuate behaviors that hamper the progress of change. Here are key signs that your systems are hindering change:

- People are penalized for making mistakes, taking risks, or moving forward with the transformation.

- Performance is measured on criteria that are not aligned with the desired results.

- Systems reward behaviors that are no longer important or relevant.

- Promotions are based on loyalty to individuals who have a lot to lose in the change.

Take the following steps to change personnel information and HR systems that are seriously at odds with the change vision:

- Ensure that performance appraisals include elements that demonstrate commitment to the vision by including competencies, behaviors, and the like during the review.

- Back up commitment with pay.

- Make promotion decisions objectively and consistently with the vision (i.e., can people break out of existing patterns and be successful?).

- Ensure that succession plans promote individuals who will support the vision and serve as role models.

- Ensure that recruiting and hiring systems select people who fit the new needs.

Resistant Leaders and Managers

Dealing with resistance from those involved with or affected by your initiative is part of any change effort. Probably the most serious challenge to successful change comes when members of leadership and management—those you're relying upon to implement the change—resist the effort. When this occurs, it's usually obvious where and why, but here are some familiar signs of change resistance within your leadership/management team:

- Withholding information or resources from those who need them.

- Undermining the credibility of those proposing and driving the change effort.

- Refusing to participate in subtle ways.

- Micromanaging the group's activities.

- Fostering a climate of political backbiting and us-versus-them.

- Treating any change effort by a team member as disloyalty.

- Controlling all decisions and incoming/outgoing communications.

It's critical that you deal clearly, sensibly, and sensitively with high-level resistance. Here are a few pointers:

- Confront resistance directly; remember, groups don't resist, individuals do.

- Engage resisters in honest discussion about their concerns.

- Provide resisters with opportunities to resolve the problems.

- Always deal with people in a fair, straightforward, and timely manner.

- For the good of the organization and the change initiative, be clear about the bottom line of behavior. Communicate immediately when resistant behavior is not acceptable, and explain the consequences.

- If alterations in leadership/management are necessary, proceed in a way that is clear, honest, direct, and timely.

You need to gauge carefully which of the preceding strategies and suggestions will be workable within the context of your specific change initiative. Those leading the change may not be ready for or capable of making all of the changes required at a particular time. If this is the case, they should focus on removing those barriers that pose the most serious or substantial challenge to the vision. This will go a long way toward enabling people to act and will demonstrate leadership's commitment to the change. If such barriers remain in place while leaders attempt to move forward on the other steps, employees will sense the tension and inconsistency, and will become skeptical of the commitment to make the change a success.

One concrete way to assess what's moving the change process forward, or holding it back, is to evaluate the specific behaviors of those involved with the initiative. The Stakeholder Behavioral Map (see assessment tool 5-1) is a simple tool to help assess change-related

Stakeholder behavioral map

Who is the stakeholder or stakeholder group?	What is the behavior?	If resistant, what is the root cause? If neutral, how might it be improved? If positive, how might it be improved further?	How is the resistance being expressed or demonstrated?	What action is to be taken?	What is the completion date?

behavior and to plan the actions needed to bust the barriers that stand in the way of success.

Encouraging Risk Taking and Innovation

Once the major barriers to change have been removed, it's up to the leaders to foster a new way of thinking and acting—to help employees break out of old behavior patterns and habits. Here are eight ways leaders can stimulate and encourage new ideas and risk taking, along with specific questions and issues to consider:

1. Encourage testing activities throughout the change process. "Piloting" ideas throughout the process provides safe opportunities to challenge traditional approaches and creates a mind-set of continuous improvement.

   - How or where could you try this now?

   - What are different ways to test whether this would work?

2. Respond constructively to failure. How leaders respond to "failure" or less successful ideas will shape the attitude toward risk taking.

   - What can you learn from this?

   - What should you do differently?

   - How can you support the individual taking the risk?

3. Encourage and support adoption of new ideas as they arise.

   - Ask continuously for input and ideas.

   - Provide opportunities for feedback.

   - Encourage first steps in new directions.

   - Reward employees for new ideas, for taking risks.

4. Challenge traditional thinking by seeking other ideas or approaches and not settling for the default option.

   - How could you do this differently?

- What would others do in this case?

- What are others doing that's working?

5. Look for best-of-breed approaches in each area of the project to provide a new framework for thinking.

   - Use a different competitor as a benchmark.

   - Consider comparing your company to a different industry or country.

   - Identify new metrics as benchmarks.

6. Create a sense of fun. Change creates uncertainty and anxiety. People react to change by retreating to their comfortable habits and making safe decisions, or by lashing out in defense of familiar ways. By creating a relaxed atmosphere, it is more likely that new ideas will be generated, received more openly, and acted upon.

   - Try unusual locations or settings for meetings.

   - Add some humor to communication.

   - Use analogies and metaphors to get your point across more vividly.

   - Try creative approaches for problem solving, reexamine old rationales, flip the current paradigms.

7. Generate lots of alternatives without imposing practical constraints.

   - What would be a totally radical thing to do in this case?

   - What would be the opposite of what you normally do?

   - What would it be like to actually try this?

8. Demonstrate willingness to take risks. Leaders can set the tone for risk taking by taking chances themselves.

   - Ask for input on something that is usually not open for discussion.

- Run a traditional activity in a different setting or context.

- Use a different approach to demonstrate your willingness to try new things.

- Make a symbolic gesture that is unusual and bold.

- Selectively show your own weaknesses or shortcomings.

Outcomes

If your employees have truly been enabled to take action, you should witness the following results:

- Individuals and groups receive the training, performance support, and development opportunities needed to do the work successfully.

- Key managers commit the time and resources necessary to support the effort.

- Individuals and groups assume the responsibility and possess sufficient authority to make the decisions required to turn the transformation into a reality.

- Organizational processes and systems are aligned to reward and recognize individuals whose actions are consistent with the vision, and do not punish them for constructive failures or for taking calculated and reasonable risks.

- Performance measures are aligned so that a "strategic line of sight" exists from the bottom to the top of the organization, enabling people to see how their individual performance is moving the change effort and the organization forward.

- People, process, and technological barriers have been identified and action steps taken to clear the path to achieving the transformation.

Key Implementation Challenges

Several challenges are likely to emerge when attempting to enable leaders and stakeholders to take action during a change initiative.

Keeping Leaders Focused on the Change Initiative

At this point, leaders of the organization have:

- Identified the problem.

- Begun putting the necessary guiding teams in place.

- Assisted in developing a vision.

- Communicated this vision to the stakeholders.

When leadership sees the enthusiastic response to the vision, they may be tempted to ease up and turn their attention to other priorities before real action and results are produced. Creating a viable, inspiring vision and communicating it well so that the excitement and motivation spread through the organization are significant achievements, critical to success. But the next step, removing barriers, is just as crucial. Leaders need to stay focused on the goals still ahead so they see the barriers to action and the changes that are needed. As noted earlier, if you motivate your people with a compelling vision, but don't remove the obstacles in their way, they'll start to doubt the genuineness of the change, to mistrust leadership, and eventually become discouraged or even cynical.

Removing the Barriers Fast

You can't put this off until later. When barriers are not removed promptly, people become so frustrated in their attempts to do things right that they often give up. Reenlisting their help later requires much more effort, and may even be impossible. Removing barriers to action quickly is critical to keeping the project's urgency, and your employees' energy, at high levels.

Managing Resistant Leaders

When the barrier to progress is a leader in the organization, the situation must be dealt with immediately because the organization's response to a resistant leader delivers a clear message about the firm's support of the change initiative. Moreover, allowing such a leadership problem to fester will create uncertainty and even ill will in the organization and is just another reason why the problem should be dealt with immediately. Clearly the first step is a one-on-one discussion to probe the source of resistance and attempt to obtain the leader's support. However, if repeated discussions fail to get this person on board, more drastic action must be taken if the change initiative is to succeed. As a last resort, demotion, transfer, or even termination must be considered. The action should be public so that everyone witnesses the organization's commitment to the change, as well as its resolve to remove any barriers that stand in the way of the vision.

Identifying Organizational Barriers

Most structural obstacles will seem obvious to an outsider, but people in organizations are so accustomed to their internal systems that they may not be able to see the problem, much less any alternative. In addition, the benefits of the current structure, and the potential losses if they let go of it, often appear greater and more immediate than the possible gains from changes in a seemingly distant and far-off future. In this case, change leaders must help people to step back and attain a broader perspective, one that will allow them to see why the change is for the overall good of the organization.

Gauging Effectiveness

Signs of Enablement

To gauge your success at enabling people for change, routinely ask yourself the following questions, using your group as a test:

- Am I doing what it takes to motivate my people to do the work of change?

- Am I giving my people the necessary knowledge, skills, and abilities?

- Am I providing the resources necessary to tackle the challenges and problems that emerge in the change effort?

- Have I given the right people enough authority to make sound decisions?

- Am I ensuring that all involved in the change initiative are receiving adequate support from their managers and peers?

- Have I set up the right systems to measure and reward people for their change efforts?

A primary goal of the guiding teams in this step, and a critical element in enabling action, is to ensure that rewards, performance, training, and other human capital processes and systems are aligned with the change effort. If they have been effective, you will see the following changes:

- The level of activity relating to the change increases as more people get involved.

- Participation in change-related activities becomes routine.

- The quality and quantity of feedback increases.

- Attendance at related training is high.

- Resources are freed up.

- Open, honest discussions to address conflicts and problems happen more frequently.

- Issues and problems are identified and acted upon rapidly.

- Feedback and suggestions are offered spontaneously.

- New ideas are proposed and tested.

- More informal talk about the initiative occurs.

- The change initiative becomes a regular topic on management agendas.

Alternatively, here are some warning signs that indicate you're not doing enough to identify and eliminate the barriers to change:

- There is a high level of skepticism about the change effort.

- Employees show a reluctance and/or a lack of motivation to participate.

- Instead of dealing with problems as they arise, people avoid them.

- Progress on the change initiative is too slow.

- People are frustrated and make mistakes.

- Change teams are working long hours.

- Many ideas are generated but few are acted upon.

- Decisions are recycled long after being approved.

- The decision-making process is long and involves multiple levels of approval.

- Leaders are reluctant to free up resources.

- Change efforts are given low priority.

- The dissatisfaction with performance appraisals is high.

- People give up even after being successful.

If you do not address the barriers that are impeding progress, the energy needed to move the change effort forward will disappear.

The Enabling Action Diagnostic

If individuals are to carry out the vision, they must have the motive, means, and opportunities to take action, and barriers that stand in the way must be removed. Individuals will not take action if they perceive it will lead to failure or, worse, punishment. The Enabling Action Diagnostic will help you determine the degree to which stakeholders feel that barriers are being busted.

To use the diagnostic successfully, follow these steps:

- Distribute the diagnostic (assessment tool 5-2) to individuals whose perspective is desired.

- Ask the individuals being surveyed to answer the questions according to their own experiences and knowledge of the organization.

- As indicated on the directions that accompany the diagnostic, respondents will assign a rating of 1 to 6 to each question, with 1 indicating "strongly disagree" and 6 indicating "strongly agree."

- Tally the results after the sheets have been returned to you. The farther the results are from the maximum score possible, the more urgent the problem.

Suggestions for Improvement

In successful change efforts, enabling action means making tough decisions and taking bold steps to remove obstacles that stop people from pursuing the change initiative. If the scores on this diagnostic questionnaire are low, then the way the organization goes about its work is acting as a barrier to the change effort. The following suggestions may help you remove the obstacles and encourage the risk taking and innovation needed for success.

Realign Performance Measures with the Change Initiative

Companies often create bold change initiatives but forget to modify their performance measures to align with the new behaviors.

The enabling action diagnostic

Instructions

- Please read each statement and indicate the extent to which it describes the norm in your organization as a whole. Your responses should reflect what you have experienced as well as what you have generally observed in your organization.
- Answer the questions using a 6-point scale; the far left of the scale indicates that you strongly disagree and the far right of the scale indicates that you strongly agree. Please respond by checking the box that corresponds most closely to your situation.
- If you do not know the answer, check the "Do not know" box.
- Please take the time to respond to the open-ended questions at the end of the survey. Your responses are crucial in improving the change initiative.
- Be honest in your responses. There are no right or wrong answers, and your answers will remain completely confidential.

Enabling action	Strongly disagree (1)					Strongly agree (6)	Do not know
As a member of this organization, I . . .							
1. Feel that our organizational structure makes our change initiative achievable.	☐	☐	☐	☐	☐	☐	☐
2. Feel that our leaders remove the barriers in an orderly manner to allow us to make our change effort successful.	☐	☐	☐	☐	☐	☐	☐
3. Feel that we have been given the right training/education to make us successful in the future.	☐	☐	☐	☐	☐	☐	☐
4. Feel that we have been given timely training/education.	☐	☐	☐	☐	☐	☐	☐
5. Feel that there are no barriers stopping me from behaving/performing in the new way.	☐	☐	☐	☐	☐	☐	☐
6. Believe that individuals are rewarded for behaving in ways that support our new change initiative and future goals.	☐	☐	☐	☐	☐	☐	☐
7. Feel the reward system promotes the behavior needed to make our change effort successful.	☐	☐	☐	☐	☐	☐	☐
8. Feel that people actively help each other find ways to make the change a success.	☐	☐	☐	☐	☐	☐	☐
9. Believe that leadership provides objective feedback on our progress relative to the change effort.	☐	☐	☐	☐	☐	☐	☐
10. Feel that our information systems provide us with the information we need to measure our performance against our new targets.	☐	☐	☐	☐	☐	☐	☐
11. Believe that leadership supports the type of behavior, skills, and attitudes needed to attain our change initiative.	☐	☐	☐	☐	☐	☐	☐
12. Believe that management demonstrates the type of behavior, skills, and attitudes needed to attain our change initiative.	☐	☐	☐	☐	☐	☐	☐

The enabling action diagnostic *(continued)*

Enabling action	Strongly disagree (1)					Strongly agree (6)	Do not know
13. Feel that leadership promoted our new change initiative effectively enough that individuals believe they can support it.	☐	☐	☐	☐	☐	☐	☐
14. Feel that the behavior of people in positions of power (executives, managers, supervisors) who act against the change initiative has been, or will be, corrected.	☐	☐	☐	☐	☐	☐	☐
15. Feel that leadership has removed work activities that divert us from the goals of the change initiative.	☐	☐	☐	☐	☐	☐	☐
Subtotals	x 1	+ x 2	+ x 3	+ x 4	+ x 5	+ x 6	
= Grand total							

To get your totals

Add the check marks in vertical columns to get subtotals. Multiply that total by the number at the bottom of each column. Then add the subtotals together to get the grand total.

Grand total: 15 = serious problems, 90 = no problems. Any score below a 60 indicates a need for improvement.

Open-ended feedback

1. How enabled do you feel to make change happen? Why?

_____

_____

_____

_____

_____

2. What actions have supervisors/executives/leaders taken that have helped you make the change happen?

_____

_____

_____

_____

_____

3. What actions have supervisors/executives/leaders taken that have obstructed change?

_____

_____

_____

_____

_____

(continued)

The enabling action diagnostic *(continued)*

4. What barriers impede your progress toward achieving the change?

_____
_____
_____
_____
_____

5. What would help you support the change effort?

_____
_____
_____
_____
_____

6. What has the organization done to make you feel a part of the change effort?

_____
_____
_____
_____
_____

Employees should be rewarded, formally or informally, for acting on the change initiative. Misalignment of the performance measurement system and the change initiative can cause employees to stick to old habits or, worse, can punish them for their change efforts.

Ensure that Leaders Are on the Same Page

Nothing is more dangerous or destructive to a change initiative than leaders who do not demonstrate support or who actively work against the change. Make sure that you're communicating closely with your managers and leaders, so that they not only agree with the change initiative, but actively work to reinforce the vision. Talk to them frequently about why they must provide an environment where employees are rewarded for change. As stated earlier, if a manager or executive proves inflexible in opposition to the change, it's imperative to either convert or remove this person and resolve the tension so that the change can proceed.

Enable People with Training and Better Information Systems

Change efforts usually involve people learning new ways to do their job. This often throws employees into a state of uncertainty and can potentially create a lack of confidence in themselves and in the change effort. Providing employees with effective, timely, and relevant training increases their confidence in their own skills and makes them more likely to support the change. Furthermore, creating new information systems and norms specifically around the change effort will reduce uncertainty as well as resistance due to poor or scarce information.

Communicating in This Step

Communicating and getting feedback is particularly crucial in this step, since identifying and removing organizational barriers often leads into sensitive territory. When familiar ways of doing things are threatened, people's territory is broached, and it's imperative for leaders to be clear, direct, timely, and as transparent as possible in their communications. Here are some additional communication goals change leaders should focus on during this stage:

- Broaden the guiding teams' communication efforts in order to foster dialogue and enlist the help of as many parts of the organization as possible.

- Encourage new ideas by communicating success stories, results of new activities, and support and recognition for efforts and sacrifices.

- Communicate the lessons learned from less successful attempts, while also supporting the individuals involved.

- Ensure that creative ideas and suggestions are captured and acted on.

- Continue to communicate the overarching need and vision for change.

Stories to Remember from Step 5 of *The Heart of Change*

Use the following story summaries and questions to help you eliminate barriers to change.

"Retooling the Boss"

Joe was a loyal employee, but he always responded to customer requests by saying what they wanted couldn't be done, or the request had been discussed and decided against. This became such a problem that one of the company's best customers demanded that Joe be terminated. But the leader had a better idea—have Joe go to work for the customer, at the company's expense, for six months. When Joe resisted, his leader told him he had two options: go to work for the customer or leave the company. Becoming a quality inspector for the customer required Joe to change. Joe found that several of the products that he always thought were high quality were actually not meeting the customer's needs, and he voiced these concerns and made recommendations for modifying them. When he returned to the company after six months, he was a proponent of change and one of the best managers in the company.

(Summarized from *The Heart of Change,* pages 104–106)

- Which leaders need to change their perspective so that they are enabling the change effort rather than hindering it?

- What efforts are being made to bring middle management on board?

- What is being done to understand the fundamental reasons for barriers?

- Are these barriers different than what you originally thought?

"The Worldwide Competition"

Leadership of this company knew they were capable of making big advancements, but employees would always say that even minor changes were difficult. To help them see that the company was capable of greater achievements, leadership created a worldwide competition with an impressive recognition program. Teams registered to enter the competition and then began working on their improvement ideas. After several rounds of judging, the finalists were brought to an exotic holiday spot to present their ideas to the management team. In an energetic concluding ceremony, all teams were acknowledged and winners were announced. The first year, two thousand people were involved in the competition, but by year three, the number grew to nine thousand participants. This competition has created an environment in which individuals are empowered and are consistently achieving large-scale breakthroughs.

(Summarized from *The Heart of Change,* pages 109–111)

- What creative recognition programs are in place to foster dramatic improvements?

- How can you stage your recognition so that it makes people want to be part of the drama?

- How do you avoid the perception of "manipulating the organization" to get what you want?

"Making Movies on the Factory Floor"

Tim, a division executive, informed plant leadership that senior management would no longer conduct inspections at the plant. Instead, it was important to enable the workforce to make recommendations for improvement. After several months of trying different things, they decided to videotape workers through the production cycle of a product and then show these tapes to the workers. While watching the tape, workers began noticing opportunities for improvement for the first time. Because of the success of the initial videotapes, they became a regular method for identifying improvements.

(Summarized from *The Heart of Change*, pages 117–120)

- How can you get people to see for themselves how to improve?

- What feedback processes are in place for self-improvement?

- Do your employees have the right tools to enable action and, more important, what are you doing to ensure they know how to use them?

"Harold and Lidia"

After identifying a few barriers that they had control over, Harold and Lidia conducted an off-site meeting with representatives from their department. In this meeting they focused on what they were collectively doing to stomp on new ideas and agreed to help each other stop this behavior. In the three months following the meeting they worked together to come up with a number of new ideas, one of which proved to be promising. In short, they chose issues they could impact and focused on a few at a time.   (Summarized from *The Heart of Change*, pages 121–122)

- Are people working on barriers that they can influence and feel are critical to eliminate?

- What actions are the guiding teams taking to support "barrier busting"?

- How motivated are the teams to bust barriers? How successful are they?

More Resources

Argyris, Chris. **Knowledge for Action: A Guide to Overcoming Barriers to Organizational Change**. San Francisco: Jossey-Bass, 1993.

> Argyris demonstrates how "actionable knowledge" can be produced and presents a step-by-step description of how to evaluate an organization's capacity to learn, analyze the data, and design and implement effective interventions that help change the status quo and create a more dynamic and innovative organization.

Axelrod, Richard H. **Terms of Engagement: Changing the Way We Change Organizations**. New York: Berrett-Koehler Publishers, 2000.

> Axelrod presents a new paradigm for successful change based on developing an engaged organization by widening the circle of involvement, connecting people to each other, creating communities of action, and practicing democratic principles.

Block, Peter. **The Empowered Manager: Positive Political Skills at Work**. San Francisco: Jossey-Bass, 1987.

> Managers have difficulty leading change when they feel stifled by bureaucracy and powerless to control their own destinies. Block presents ways to treat all members of the organization as entrepreneurs so that employees feel that they are playing an active role in creating an organization of their own choosing.

Collins, James C., and Porras, Jerry I. **Built to Last: Successful Habits of Visionary Companies**. New York: Perseus Books, 1997.

> In this work, Collins discusses how successful companies create a safe environment for experimentation and how this atmosphere, combined with flexibility and shared ideology, is critical to enabling a workforce to implement change.

Galbraith, Jay, Downey, Diane, and Kates, Amy. **Designing Dynamic Organizations: A Hands-on Guide for Leaders at All Levels**. New York: AMACOM, 2001.

> Based on Galbraith's world-renowned star model approach, this book includes examples and worksheets that guide readers through the essential steps of organizational design and how it enables firms to transform themselves and overcome the barriers inherent in organizational processes.

Pasmore, William A. **Creating Strategic Change: Designing the Flexible, High-Performing Organization**. New York: John Wiley & Sons, 1994.

> For an organization to succeed in an environment of ever-accelerating change, traditional hierarchies must be replaced with a new breed of flexible, high-performance organization structures capable of adapting to the changes that occur both within the firm and in the marketplace.

Senge, Peter M. **The Fifth Discipline: The Art and Practice of the Learning Organization**. New York: Doubleday/Currency, 1994.

> In the knowledge economy, people are the only long-term competitive advantage an organization has. Senge explains how maximizing their value requires establish-

ing a learning organization and providing continuous opportunities for lifelong learning.

Senge, Peter M., Roberts, Charlotte, Ross, Richard B., and Smigh, Bryan. **The Fifth Discipline Fieldbook: Strategies and Tools for Building a Learning Organization.** New York: Doubleday/Currency, 1994.

Senge provides stories and hands-on guidance for reinventing relationships, being loyal to the truth, building a shared vision, organizing as a community, and designing an organization's governing ideas.

Shafritz, Jay M., and Ott, J. Steven. **Classics of Organization Theory**. Belmont: Wadsworth, 2000.

This volume contains the most important works in organization theory from the most influential authors in the field. These works have withstood the test of time, and the ideas presented are commonly referenced in the study of organizational theory.

Ulrich, Dave, and Lake, Dale. **Organizational Capability**. New York: Perseus Books, 1997.

It has been said that the people are a company's most important asset, but in this work the authors go beyond this premise by introducing "organizational capability" as a concept to help companies realize their potential from the inside out.

Wenger, Etienne C., Pfeffer, Jeffrey, Sutton, Robert I., Duguid, Paul, and Brown, John Seely. **Harvard Business Review on Organizational Learning**. Boston: Harvard Business School Publishing, 2001.

In this volume of the **Harvard Business Review** series, the authors analyze the factors impacting learning and knowledge management in organizations and offer better strategies for fostering organizational learning.

Create Short-Term Wins

In successful change efforts, empowered people create short-term wins—victories that nourish faith in the change effort, emotionally reward the hard workers, keep the critics at bay, and build momentum. Without sufficient wins that are visible, timely, unambiguous, and meaningful to others, change efforts inevitably run into serious problems.

—from Step 6 of *The Heart of Change*

Purpose

Short-term wins that are timely, visible, and meaningful are critical to building the credibility needed to sustain the change effort over time. Without tangible evidence that the effort is paying off, stakeholders grow wary that the initiative is absorbing too many resources and skeptics become increasingly difficult to convince. In addition, the enthusiasm of those involved wanes as they wonder if their sacrifices are worth the effort. All of this results in declining urgency and a loss of crucial momentum.

In concrete terms, short-term wins provide these benefits:

- Evidence that the plan for change is working.

- A test against real conditions and an opportunity to adjust the plan.

- Tangible results to help keep leaders and stakeholders on board as well as undermine resisters and silence the cynics.

- A chance to catch your breath and celebrate—to make a tough journey more tolerable.

Approach

You can get the most benefit out of short-term wins by taking the following four steps:

1. Planning for visible improvements in performance.

2. Achieving those wins.

3. Communicating the wins visibly and convincingly.

4. Embedding the learning into the plan going forward.

Planning for Visible Improvements in Performance

Delivering short-term results in a change effort, whether it spans just a few months or several years, can be a challenge. Overly ambitious targets can heavily tax scarce resources as well as divert attention from the real objectives. On the other hand, targets that are too easy provide ammunition for skeptics who are already questioning the value of the effort. Effective short-term wins require careful planning in order to strike the right balance.

In scanning the landscape for the right "low-hanging fruit," use the following characteristics as a guide for determining what will make the most effective short-term wins:

- *Measurable:* Vague or fuzzy advances won't help you make the case for change. To be convincing, performance improvements must be clear and concrete.

- *Visible:* People in the organization need to see real evidence of the progress and the validity of the change effort.

- *Timely:* Ideally, results should appear within a ninety-day timeframe, and on a rolling basis.

- *Relevant to all stakeholders:* The wins should be valuable to customers, employees, shareholders, and leaders of the organization.

- *Relevant to the objectives:* Wins should be clearly related to the change effort so as to build support for the work still ahead.

- *Relevant to the situation:* Wins should provide a test of the vision and change plan against real conditions so they can provide useful data to adjust the plan.

- *Relevant to the people:* Wins should involve the people who need to carry the change forward.

Achieving Wins

First, you need to plan and identify potential short-term wins; then you must make them happen. While members of the senior guiding team have until now been the primary actors in creating vision, strategies, and plans, it is the field guiding teams and people who work in the business process/functional areas who must actually develop and implement the short-term wins. To do so they must complete several key steps:

- Conduct workshops to identify short-term wins.

- Build specific tasks and goals into the project plans and budgets.

- Give clear accountabilities for implementing the short-term wins.

- Assign responsibilities within the guiding teams for monitoring the efforts.

- Ensure that measurement systems allow management to track key data and demonstrate improvements.

The matrix in assessment tool 6-1 can help determine which short-term wins will significantly affect the momentum of the workforce. After brainstorming a list of potential short-term wins, evaluate each based on the ease of implementation and the size of the payoff, and plot the results in the matrix. Efforts should focus on short-term wins that are the easiest to achieve with the biggest payoff ("Home Runs"). You may also choose to target some of the easy ones that have a smaller payoff ("Base Hits") if they will not interfere with more important work. I've used a baseball metaphor here for

ASSESSMENT TOOL 6-1

Short-term wins payoff matrix

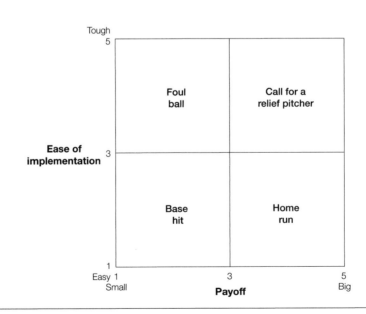

clarity and simplicity (and a little fun), but use whatever imagery you like that is most communicative and relevant to your situation.

Once you have determined which short-term wins are worth pursuing, you will need to establish the steps necessary for implementation, determine owners and accountabilities, and set due dates. Assessment tool 6-2 is a useful template to help prepare for implementation, seek approval from leadership, and roll out short-term wins.

Communicating Wins Visibly and Convincingly

As with the larger step 4 challenge of communicating for buy-in, you must immediately communicate achievement of short-term wins to all the relevant parties.

ASSESSMENT TOOL 6-2

Short-term wins planning template

Foul ball	Call for a relief pitcher	Issue:		
Base hit	Home run	Recommendation:		
Action step			**Owner**	**Due date**

Outcome description:

Guiding team leader(s):	Owner(s):

Status: Approved   Declined   Pending   Resolution date:

The key *objectives* of communicating wins are:

- To gain credibility.

- To build support for the effort.

- To demonstrate that progress is occurring.

Therefore, the targeted *audiences* should be everybody from whom you seek support:

- The leaders who provide resources to the effort.

- The people in the organization who will be affected by the change.

- The skeptics, so they become believers.

- The supporters, so they become active participants.

The key *messages* must include:

- Communicating enthusiasm and excitement about achievements and progress.

- Clarifying how the wins are related to the change effort.

- Demonstrating how the wins prove the validity of the vision.

- Communicating progress without giving the impression that the work is complete.

- Demonstrating unequivocal positive results that leave little room for doubt that progress is being made.

Effective *mechanisms* for delivering the messages are:

- A key sponsor for the change.

- A member of a guiding team.

- A former resister to the change.

- A satisfied or impressed customer.

- A system that provides reliable data.

- A trial test that can be seen.

Embedding the Learning into the Plan

Short-term results (positive or negative) will provide useful information about the validity of the vision and the feasibility of the change effort. The results might answer the following questions and thereby guide the shape and direction of the change effort:

- Are the project targets and objectives achievable? Realistic?

- Is the vision too bold? Too conservative?

- Is the change plan working? What is the key evidence of that?

- Does the plan address all key areas? Are there any missing components?

- Are the effort estimates accurate? Where should less or more time be spent?

- What should be done to sustain achievements to date?

- What should be done to ensure further success?

- What should be done differently based on the failure?

- What one thing would have improved the results?

- What should be stopped?

- Who should be given more responsibility?

- Who should be removed from the initiative?

Outcomes

With a critical mass of the right short-terms wins, the organization should gain:

- Confidence that they have a change plan based on concrete evidence, one in which the desired changes are feasible and based on a valid vision.

- Support from people in positions of power or influence.

- Momentum for the change effort, with more people becoming active supporters and helpers.

- Guiding teams with renewed motivation for the task, inspiring others to act.

- A sense of excitement as people *see* change happening, *feel* the momentum, and want to *act*.

Key Implementation Challenges

While the idea of short-term wins and low-hanging fruit often implies that the wins will be easy, this is not always so. The right people have to take the time to identify what tasks are redundant, frustrating, unnecessary, and so forth. These individuals are usually the ones who actually do the work, as they know what activities can be eliminated, modified, or transferred to another area in the organization. The following challenges are likely to emerge as you attempt to bolster your change effort with smaller accomplishments along the way.

Explaining Short-Term Efforts Failures

Much value and learning can be gained from a failure to achieve targeted short-term results. But the effect can be devastating for the initiative. Unfortunately, bad news travels faster than good, has a much stronger emotional effect, and tends to leave a lasting impression.

The focus of the communication effort in these cases is therefore in damage control. The following tips may prove useful:

- Emphasize the exploratory nature of short-term wins.

- Describe the lessons learned and how they helped with the change effort.

- Clarify the implications for the team and the vision.

- Avoid laying blame but credit the people involved for their effort.

Balancing Goals with Short- and Long-Term Payoffs

Balancing both short- and long-term demands requires carefully planning resources and managing priorities. A typical mistake made by guiding teams is to attack the long-term objectives with lengthy initiatives, but fail to plan for shorter-term achievements. Then, in response to increased pressure for results from stakeholders, they suddenly focus all their effort on producing short-term wins. Eventually, they have to rekindle the momentum behind the longer-term activities, leaving the organization confused. This situation can be avoided by devoting the necessary attention to step 3, getting the vision right, and including both short- and long-term perspectives when developing the performance measures needed to determine success.

Gauging Effectiveness

Characteristics of Effective Short-Term Wins

Short-term wins reinforce the change effort by providing "proof" that progress is being made toward achieving the vision. This progress actually recharges the sense of urgency, keeping emotions high and resistance low. It's the short-term wins that get the "doubting Toms" to acknowledge that the change is taking root. The following are some indicators of effective short-term wins:

- Change efforts are balanced between short-term wins and long-term results.

- Discussion occurs among internal and external stakeholders concerning the tangible results.

- People talk about the vision as something achievable.

- Support for the change grows among those employees and managers who will be affected by the change as well as leaders who will need to champion the effort.

- Some resisters become supporters.

- Some supporters become active helpers.

- Key influencers use results of short-term wins to demonstrate the feasibility of achieving the vision.

- Important achievements are recognized and celebrated.

- The guiding teams thrive on renewed energy.

The Short-Term Wins Diagnostic

Without tangible evidence that the effort is paying off, leaders often become concerned that the initiative is merely absorbing resources without effecting positive change. Participant enthusiasm begins to wane as they wonder if their sacrifices are worth the effort. Skeptics become increasingly difficult to stave off, let alone convince that the effort is worthy. In short, a series of quick wins are critical to keep up the urgency of the change initiative. This tool will help you determine the effectiveness of the short-term wins associated with your change effort.

To use the diagnostic successfully, follow these steps:

- Distribute the Short-Term Wins Diagnostic (assessment tool 6-3) to individuals whose perspective is desired.

The short-term wins diagnostic

Instructions

- Please read each statement and indicate the extent to which it describes the norm in your organization as a whole. Your responses should reflect what you have experienced as well as what you have generally observed in your organization.
- Answer the questions using a 6-point scale; the far left of the scale indicates that you strongly disagree and the far right of the scale indicates that you strongly agree. Please respond by checking the box that corresponds most closely to your situation.
- If you do not know the answer, check the "Do not know" box.
- Please take the time to respond to the open-ended questions at the end of the survey. Your responses are crucial in improving the change initiative.
- Be honest in your responses. There are no right or wrong answers, and your answers will remain completely confidential.

Short-term wins	Strongly disagree (1)					Strongly agree (6)	Do not know
As a member of this organization, I . . .							
1. Have seen clear evidence that the change effort is working.	☐	☐	☐	☐	☐	☐	☐
2. Am motivated to pursue the long-term success of the effort because of recent short-term successes.	☐	☐	☐	☐	☐	☐	☐
3. Believe that the change effort has momentum.	☐	☐	☐	☐	☐	☐	☐
4. Feel a sense of urgency to achieve the next milestone.	☐	☐	☐	☐	☐	☐	☐
5. Have seen improvements and/or successes as a result of the change effort within the first six months.	☐	☐	☐	☐	☐	☐	☐
6. Have seen improvements and/or successes as a result of the change effort within the first twelve months.	☐	☐	☐	☐	☐	☐	☐
7. Work toward planned milestones that support our change initiative.	☐	☐	☐	☐	☐	☐	☐
8. Have celebrated the organization's success as we've hit major milestones.	☐	☐	☐	☐	☐	☐	☐
9. Have been reinforced/rewarded for meeting milestones.	☐	☐	☐	☐	☐	☐	☐
10. Believe that the milestones we've hit have produced successes that are visible to the entire organization.	☐	☐	☐	☐	☐	☐	☐
11. Believe that the milestones we've hit have produced successes that are visible to my department.	☐	☐	☐	☐	☐	☐	☐
12. Clearly believe that the successes we've achieved are related to the change effort.	☐	☐	☐	☐	☐	☐	☐
13. Believe that the sacrifices our change initiative requires are worth it.	☐	☐	☐	☐	☐	☐	☐

(continued)

The short-term wins diagnostic *(continued)*

Short-term wins	Strongly disagree (1)					Strongly agree (6)	Do not know
14. Believe that our successes have either justified our change initiative or provided us with the data we needed to improve it.	☐	☐	☐	☐	☐	☐	☐
15. Feel that resisters to the change effort have been won over by some of the visible successes we've achieved.	☐	☐	☐	☐	☐	☐	☐
16. Understand that, without short-term wins, we cannot achieve the results that we're after.	☐	☐	☐	☐	☐	☐	☐
Subtotals	x 1	+ x 2	+ x 3	+ x 4	+ x 5	+ x 6	
= Grand total							

To get your totals

Add the check marks in vertical columns to get subtotals. Multiply that total by the number at the bottom of each column. Then add the subtotals together to get the grand total.

Grand total: 15 = serious problems, 90 = no problems. Any score below a 60 indicates a need for improvement.

Open-ended feedback

1. What short-term wins, or improvements, would you like to see as a result of our change effort?

_____

_____

_____

_____

_____

2. Have the successes we've achieved been visible enough? If not, how would you suggest that we make them more visible?

_____

_____

_____

_____

_____

3. Are we achieving enough short-term wins to keep up the momentum?

_____

_____

_____

_____

_____

ASSESSMENT TOOL 6-3

The short-term wins diagnostic *(continued)*

4. What short-term wins do you recall the organization achieving?

_____
_____
_____
_____
_____

5. What short-term wins have been most personally rewarding to you?

_____
_____
_____
_____
_____

6. How have these short-term wins impacted your thoughts or behavior around the change effort?

_____
_____
_____
_____
_____

- Ask the individuals being surveyed to answer the questions according to their own experiences and knowledge of the organization.

- As indicated on the directions that accompany the diagnostic, respondents will assign a rating of 1 to 6 to each question, with 1 indicating "strongly disagree" and 6 indicating "strongly agree."

- Tally the results after the sheets have been returned to you. The farther the results are from the maximum score possible, the more pressing the problem.

Suggestions for Improvement

Change of any magnitude is never universally popular. There will always be skeptics who think that the changes will hurt or even lead to the downfall of your organization. The best and sometimes the only way to convince those skeptics and keep supporters motivated is to celebrate and communicate the short-term successes and milestones that you have reached during the change process. If the diagnostic scores were low, regardless of whether or not your change effort is actually achieving results, people are not *seeing* the results of the change process and cannot feel the sense of excitement and pride in the changing organization. By generating short-term successes, you will be able to gain more supporters, create more excitement, and build momentum for the change effort. The following suggestions may help your organization achieve this goal.

Make Short-Term Wins Unambiguous

If people can argue about the success of a short-term win, the power of the win may be undercut. A win is always more useful when the facts are unambiguous. Many times, subtle but important improvements in various aspects of the organization are supported by cold, hard facts: increased customer satisfaction rates, increased productivity rates, increased revenue, decreased development time, or increased percentage of on-time delivery. It is important, however, to resist the temptation to stretch the facts. This can cause more harm than good in the long run.

Make Short-Term Wins Visible

If those involved in your change effort scored low on this questionnaire, but you are certain significant progress has been made, your short-term wins are not visible enough or sufficiently linked to people's daily experience and goals. Early successes should be as "in your face" as possible and should speak to people's immediate priorities or needs. For instance, a jump in profits is a great win, but has little impact on the software development staff. A good communication plan should be able to make the wins "in your face" as well as demonstrate how all personnel can benefit from a short-term win. This is where communication can and should get creative, to really *show* how exciting the change effort can be.

Plan Your Wins

Effective, visible, unambiguous wins should be carefully planned because the right kinds of wins rarely happen spontaneously. Although the vision should guide the long-term goals of the organization, incremental steps are often approached more haphazardly, or not considered at all. While planning the change effort, be sure to build in wins that will demonstrate progress toward the overall goal. The major step in this process is to decide which wins to target first. The ideal target meets three criteria: it's fast, easy, and speaks directly to powerful constituencies. Target results rather than activities, and make sure that you can make the wins happen in a timely way. Letting too much time elapse can be deadly. For example, if an organization is attempting to improve customer satisfaction to 99 percent, waiting for full attainment of this goal before rewarding employees would likely prove ineffective. Instead, build incremental steps into the action plan, beginning with public rewards for those displaying exemplary customer service, so that people will not only see progress but feel its effects as well.

Communicating in This Step

I've mentioned several times in this chapter that it is just as important to broadly communicate short-term wins as it is to actually make them happen. The whole purpose of this step is to let people see that the change initiative is working and progressing so that urgency is sustained at a level high enough to overcome fear, anger, and complacency. Keep in mind that, even if you are actually achieving short-term wins, if no one in the organization knows it, you're not successfully executing this step. More specific communication efforts in this step should focus on seeking feedback from detractors and evaluating your communication process.

Seek Feedback from Resisters

A common mistake at this stage is to believe that by simply communicating news about short-term wins, showing everyone the "truth" about the change, you have done enough to win over skeptics and resisters. Often however, people are selective about the information they receive and choose to take in only that information which validates their own beliefs. It's important to go beyond mere broadcasting of positive results to understanding the source of their resistance by engaging them in discussion or seeking opportunities to include their point of view.

Evaluate the Effectiveness of the Communication Effort

With tangible results to communicate, this is the ideal time to evaluate the effectiveness of the communication process. A useful evaluation provides information about how well the process has:

- Cascaded information accurately.

- Created the desired beliefs.

- Generated the desired actions.

- Captured and responded to feedback.

Stories to Remember from Step 6 of *The Heart of Change*

Use the following story summaries and questions to help you develop and communicate short-term wins.

"The List on the Bulletin Boards"

When undergoing large-scale change, the temptation is to begin working on too many things at one time. To avoid this lure, Ross Kao's organization opted to focus on only four goals at a time, and they posted those goals on visible bulletin boards across the company. Once a goal was achieved, it was removed from the list and a new one was added. Because there was regular movement on the boards, the workforce saw momentum and felt the energy.

(Summarized from *The Heart of Change,* pages 128–129)

- Are your short-term wins focused?

- Are people aware of the wins?

- Do they see them as being timely, meaningful, and visible?

- What kind of bulletin board would work in your organization?

"Creating the New Navy"

Rear Admiral John Totushek described the U.S. Navy and Naval Reserve's cultural and management challenges of working more closely together, which grew in importance with the shrinking of the active force. Historically, those in the active navy viewed reservists as inferior and struggled with trusting them to handle important tasks. In order to move past these perceptions and work better together as one navy, they developed criteria for visible and meaningful short-term wins to improve the relationship, and then evaluated all possible actions against the criteria. After implementing some of the short-term wins, the stakeholders began to notice a difference in as little as thirty days and began believing the "one navy" vision was achievable.

(Summarized from *The Heart of Change,* pages 130–133)

- Have you developed criteria for short-term wins?

- How do these criteria relate to the selection of projects you plan to work on?

- Will your first win come fast enough?

"Hoopla"

Twenty-four months into a large-scale technology and process implementation, the organization was feeling the pain without seeing the gains, and those leading the effort were under pressure to show some successes. The project team initiated a "message of the week" to highlight successes, but wins were exaggerated to counteract the negative talk about the project. As a result, the communication quickly turned into project propaganda that was challenged and doubted by stakeholders.

(Summarized from *The Heart of Change*, pages 137–139)

- Are your wins really seen as wins?

- What do you need to do to make sure your wins are unambiguous?

- What are you doing to ensure you avoid "hoopla"—exaggerated claims of progress—during your change effort?

"The Senator Owned a Trucking Company"

Ron Bingham, the Governor's assistant, needed to gain support for the state government change program he was leading, so he decided to *get input* from one of the state senators who happened to own a trucking company. The senator quickly pinpointed several annual state forms that were sticking points for him because they required redundant information. When Ron requested that his change team redesign these forms, they did not immediately understand why they should shift gears to make such small changes when they already had important goals. Ron explained how this win would help them gain support from influential people, like the senator. In a short time, the team was able to reduce the fifteen forms to just one, and the senator, as well as other state government officials turned into the biggest supporters of the change program because they saw movement that was important to them.

(Summarized from *The Heart of Change*, pages 135–136)

- Have you given the proper attention to prioritizing your short-term wins?

- How are you leveraging your short-term wins to keep urgency up?

More Resources

Kotter, John P. "Leading Change: Why Transformation Efforts Fail." **Harvard Business Review**, March 1995.

> In this **HBR** article, Kotter first presents the eight-step change approach for successful corporate transformations.

Pande, Peter S., Neuman, Robert P. And Cavanagh, Roland R. **The Six Sigma Way: How GE, Motorola, and Other Top Companies Are Honing Their Performance.** New York: McGraw-Hill, 2000.

> Pande's guide offers tools and professional recommendations for implementing Six Sigma in any industry. In addition, it contains success stories from recognized organizations such as GE and Motorola, detailing how these companies have achieved major cost savings and made significant strides in quality.

Rothwell, William J., King, Stephen B., and Hohne, Carolyn K. **Human Performance Improvement: Building Practitioner Competence.** New York: Butterworth-Heinemann, 2000.

> Rothwell's Human Performance Improvement (HPI) approach helps organizations achieve quick results by focusing on improvements in intellectual capital, profitability, productivity, safety, and equity. Providing the tools and techniques to achieve a higher-performing workforce, HPI demonstrates how to assess gaps in performance, create plans for growth, develop appropriate actions for closing gaps in performance, and interpret trends.

Schaffer, Robert H. **Breakthrough Strategy: Using Short-Term Successes to Build the High-Performance Organization.** New York: Harper Business, 1988.

> Schaffer asserts that organizations can make significant productivity improvements by completing short-term "breakthrough" projects. By redirecting misused resources, a company can achieve quick, significant results that will help them move closer to their strategic vision and objectives. This how-to book provides thorough case studies of top companies' quick-hit opportunities that helped them jump-start their long-term strategic gains and gave them the impetus to move forward.

Schaffer, Robert H., and Thomson, Harvey A. "Successful Change Programs Begin with Results." **Harvard Business Review**, Jan. 1992.

> Many corporate change programs have limited success because far more focus is placed on activity rather than results. With no connection between action and outcome, momentum suffers and little real change is made. This article prescribes "results-driven" approaches that focus on achieving specific, measurable goals.

Watkins, Michael D. "New Leadership Role? Get Early Wins." **Harvard Business Review**, Sep. 1999.

In this article, the author, an associate professor at Harvard Business School, discusses what it takes to make a successful transition to a new leadership role and why quick wins are an essential part of creating credibility as a leader.

PART III

Implementing and Sustaining the Change

A S I HAVE WORKED WITH CLIENTS ON transformation initiatives throughout the years, I have heard variations of the following speech during postimplementation project celebrations:

"Team, I am so proud of all of the work you have done. For months we have been saying there is light at the end of the tunnel, and now we have finally made it to the other side. Now we can all sit back, take a deep breath, and relax!"

Following moments like this, project team members go back to their regular jobs and leaders undertake new projects. Six months later, when the organization is back to square one, leadership and project team members look around dazed and confused, saying things like: "But the implementation was so successful! What happened?"

What they failed to recognize is that the road does not end on the other side of the tunnel. By taking their eyes off the project before the new behaviors were ingrained in the organization, they left all of their hard work at the end of the tunnel while the organization made a U-turn, returning to what was comfortable. This occurs when leaders and team members:

- Assume that because a change is technically complete, their job is over.

- Take on new initiatives that remove their focus from the project they worked so hard to achieve.

- Believe everyone else shares their level of understanding and capability.

- Underestimate the learning curve and performance dip that is inevitable—even in the most perfectly planned and implemented initiative.

Steps 7 (don't let up) and 8 (make change stick) remind us of the importance to keep urgency up in order to sustain the implemented change. As you read these final two steps, think about how the first six steps can help sustain the change you worked so hard to achieve.

Don't Let Up

After the first set of short-term wins, a change effort will have direction and momentum. In successful situations, people build on this momentum to make a vision a reality by keeping urgency up and a feeling of false pride down; by eliminating unnecessary, exhausting, and demoralizing work; and by not declaring victory prematurely.

—from Step 7 of *The Heart of Change*

Purpose

The momentum created by short-term wins often propels the change effort forward, and enables stakeholders to tackle the bigger and deeper changes that will deliver the real benefits. However, it is essential to recognize the dangers that can follow short-term successes, and to realize that the change process can still fail to take root. It is not unusual for leaders to lose focus at this point, to celebrate prematurely and relax rather than redouble their efforts. Thus, the challenge for leaders in this step is twofold: to continue conveying their drive and commitment to employees and managers in order to sustain action through full implementation of the change, and to monitor and measure progress on a consistent basis. In other words, don't let up! Leaders need to stay focused and demonstrate that they are not easing the pressure to achieve the vision in which they have invested so much energy.

Approach

As leaders continue to pressure and motivate the employees involved in the change effort, they should use an approach that supports the following primary goals:

1. Leverage the momentum and credibility gained from short-term wins to consolidate gains, to learn what's working, to further refine and coordinate different aspects of the effort, and then move on to bigger parts of the change.

2. Align and monitor key organizational areas.

3. Get the people part of the equation right in order to maintain the momentum of the change.

4. Ensure the change is reaching all levels in the organization and seek feedback on its effectiveness.

5. Sustain the involvement and support of leaders.

Tackling the Bigger Change—Regroup, Refine, Coordinate

Achieving several short-term wins enables leaders and employees to:

- Consolidate gains and move forward more wisely and confidently. To accomplish this, the following questions may be helpful:
    - ✓ What lessons did we learn from the short-terms wins?
    - ✓ How can these lessons influence the future direction of the change?

- Change all systems that don't fit the new vision. Focus on the issues that are more difficult, lengthy, and risky, but that will produce more fundamental changes to the organization, such as:
  - ✓ *Processes:* How should processes, work practices, procedures, and policies be changed to fit the vision?
  - ✓ *Structure:* What accountabilities need to be realigned with the new processes?
  - ✓ *Technology:* What information is needed to sustain the new business environment? What technology is needed to enable the new processes?

Coordinate the changes to make them "fit together." Change in an organization does not happen in isolation—a change in one part of the organization reverberates in many other parts. Suddenly, the pieces may not fit together any more. While this may require a reexamination of the entire organizational system, such a process also opens the door for new opportunities. Leaders who think of their organization as an open, dynamic system are more likely to accomplish complex change because they are more apt to see and understand the sometimes subtle and complex organizational barriers that must be eliminated to bring about successful change.

Aligning and Monitoring the Organization

Figure 7-1 illustrates the systemic nature of an organizational transformation, showing one view of how organizational structure, technology, processes, measurement and rewards, and people all interact to convert vision and strategy into business performance. All of these facets of the organization's infrastructure need to be in alignment for change to be successful. Many organizations focus on replacing technology and modifying processes, and leave out the other components. Consequently, management systems often mea-

FIGURE 7-1

Framework for organizational transformation

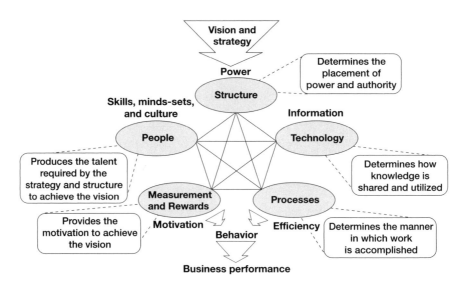

Source: Adapted from Jay R. Galbraith, *Designing Organizations* (San Francisco: Jossey Bass, 1995).

sure and reward performance that is inconsistent with the results sought, the workforce lacks the competencies to deal with the new environment, and accountabilities don't align with the targets. To achieve and sustain long-term results, you need to monitor key aspects of the organization and its infrastructure to ensure that barriers have been removed and progress is being made. Assessment tool 7-1 provides a useful way to monitor these different areas as you progress in your change effort.

Getting the People Right to Maintain Momentum

Former Israeli general and prime minister Ehud Barak once said that you make two key assessments of a person, one when they join your unit (or are hired), and another when you're in combat with them. The same rule applies in organizations. After notching a few

ASSESSMENT TOOL 7-1

Monitoring key organizational areas

Key enabling areas	Questions to uncover possible conflicts
Work design and structure	• Are roles and responsibilities aligned with the new processes? • Are the roles and responsibilities flexible enough to allow people to adjust to the new ways of doing things? • Does the work environment encourage change?
Demands from managers	• Are new expectations clear to managers? • Do they understand what's new, changed, or not required anymore? • Are they clear about their boundaries?
Performance measurement	• Do the performance measures track desired behaviors?
Rewards and recognition systems (formal and informal)	• Do formal systems reward behaviors and achievements that are consistent with the vision? • Are there new behaviors that should also be encouraged? Others that should be discouraged? • What gets noticed by the leaders and influencers in the organization? • What gets mentioned in formal or informal situations? • On what achievements and conditions are promotions based? • Do employees value current means of rewards and recognition?
Goal setting	• Are individual goals consistent with overall objectives?
Skills and competencies	• What new skills and competencies are needed? • What skills and competencies are now redundant?
Management systems	• Do management systems measure the elements we wish to pay attention to? • Have new processes been introduced? How will they be measured?
Communication processes	• What new information and feedback needs to circulate freely?
Relationships	• Is the transformed working environment creating new patterns of interaction among individuals and departments?

short-term wins, you should have a better idea about who is moving the initiative forward, and who's holding it back. Following are some key people-related considerations for keeping up the momentum:

- Think carefully about whom you will delegate to lead the changes and to manage the projects at the lower levels.

- Consider how to energize exhausted leaders.

- Determine who should be brought in to help the team gain insight and support from key people and groups resisting the change.

- Identify which leaders need to be removed from guiding teams.

Ensuring the Change is Wide-Ranging and Effective

The key challenges of the previous steps in the change process were to prove (1) that change is necessary and (2) that it can be done. Now, as multiple projects get under way, each with the potential to impact others, the role of leaders shifts from driving the startup to engaging and guiding the organization through the change effort. Positive interactions between different groups can be energizing and constructive, of course, but large initiatives can also get bogged down rapidly by the complexity of those interactions and even paralyzed if too many people are involved in the decisions. To facilitate this process and keep up the momentum, leaders need to:

- Provide guidance so that change teams can make decisions that are consistent with the vision and ensure that multiple change initiatives are coordinated.

- Manage conflicts and priorities.

- Measure results of the initiatives and adjust or realign effort.

- Continue to remove barriers to progress.

- Remove unnecessary interdependencies between initiatives.

- Appoint a program manager to ensure that existing initiatives are coordinated and add the maximum value, and that new initiatives are aligned with the vision.

- Make timely decisions.

Sustaining the Involvement and Support of Leaders

Now more than ever, strong and consistent support and timely communications from the organization's leaders are necessary to maintain momentum. Managers take their cues from their leaders. If leaders become distracted and shift their attention elsewhere, managers will interpret this as a sign that the urgency for change has relaxed. Despite the fact that leaders may need to direct attention to new goals and initiatives, they must still provide meaningful support and remain actively involved in the change process.

Here are several key strategies to help leaders sustain the change momentum, along with questions and specific points to consider:

- *Maintain the sense of urgency.* Exploring new ways to reinforce the case for change can help strengthen the desire to achieve stated goals.

  - ✓ Can recent changes in the market or industry be used to reinforce and justify the direction the organization has set?

  - ✓ Can short-term wins be used to demonstrate the potential benefits of the overall change?

- *Promote visibility of the change effort and its successes.* Remember, your actual progress may not matter unless people know about it.

  - ✓ Communicate broadly the progress and results of the change.

  - ✓ Make highly visible gestures: promotions, large meetings, public interviews, celebrations.

- *Show commitment and support for the change through actions.* You must remain ever mindful of the need to walk the talk, ensuring that your actions are consistent with the vision.

  - ✓ Give up symbols that might remind people of the old ways and create new symbols that convey the new ways.

✓ Pay attention to who is promoted and given special assignments.

✓ Promote desired behaviors in meetings, memos, and other similar avenues.

✓ Lead by example.

✓ Conduct one-to-one coaching for direct reports focused on behavior as well as business results.

• *Ensure that those implementing the change remain in touch with the true purpose of the change.* It's important to occasionally hit the reset button and remind people of the rationale for change.

✓ Conduct meetings to get their perspectives.

✓ Conduct focus sessions to learn the perceptions of stakeholders and provide feedback to the team.

✓ Have one-on-one informal conversations to get the opinions of key stakeholders and share what you learn with the team.

• *Build commitment by connecting to critical stakeholders.* They are the people who can make or break the process.

✓ Keep everyone informed of successes and challenges.

✓ Look for informal opportunities to get their opinions.

✓ Develop the appropriate measuring and monitoring processes to demonstrate continuous progress.

✓ Show that customers are happy with the change.

✓ Demonstrate that the organization is making progress by highlighting both quantitative and qualitative results.

• *Ensure middle management support for the change.* If left out of the process for too long, or not involved *enough*, this level of management can become the biggest, and most threatening, source of resistance. Too often, managers are on the receiving end of the change, responsible for implementation and results but allowed little input into the change plan itself.

> ✓ What meaningful roles can be developed for middle management to participate in leading the change?
>
> ✓ What information do managers need to promote the change in an articulate manner?

- *Listen closely to people throughout the organization.* Collecting data provides crucial input regarding the issues and barriers to change.

> ✓ What issues and concerns do people have about the change?
>
> ✓ What problems or difficulties are they dealing with?
>
> ✓ What expectations do they have about the change?
>
> ✓ What benefits or threats do they perceive from the change?
>
> ✓ Whom do they turn to for information and reassurance?

- *Conduct a feedback/assessment process on the effectiveness of the communication about the change.* Accurate information prevents leaders from forming illusions about the organization's rate of progress.

> ✓ Have executives and members of the guiding teams conduct town hall–style meetings or brown bag lunches to get timely feedback from employees.
>
> ✓ Conduct short surveys and focus groups.
>
> ✓ Challenge leaders as to the validity of their perceptions.

- *Arrange for members of the guiding teams to experience the problems "down in the ranks."* Change leaders are often so focused on eventual success that they feel they have already thought through all the issues, and mistakenly assume there are fewer problems than people experience in reality. Establish a process that gives leaders personal experience of people's actual:

> ✓ Pace of change.

✓ Attitudes toward change.

✓ Level of motivation.

✓ Beliefs about the organization and leadership's motivation.

- *Remain intensely involved in the change effort.* You must remain involved, and show your involvement, in the continuing efforts for change. Ways to demonstrate this commitment may include:

  ✓ Participating in communication events.

  ✓ Being the first to attend training sessions.

  ✓ Informally dropping in on change team meetings and listening.

  ✓ Celebrating successes with the change team and the broader organization.

  ✓ Receiving periodic feedback from the change teams on how they are doing and how effective their leadership behaviors are.

  ✓ Helping to debrief results and lessons learned.

Outcomes

If the guiding teams have succeeded in keeping the pressure on both leaders and employees to stay involved and committed to the change effort, they will see these signs of progress:

- A reinvigorated change process that provides a sense of accomplishment and optimism.

- The addition, promotion, and development of new people to help with all the changes.

- Sustained leadership from senior people who reinforce the need for change and are perceived as actively involved with the change initiative.

- A strong and continuing focus on achieving a high level of performance.

- A clear and unwavering focus on the change priorities.

Key Implementation Challenges

"Don't let up" is a clear and simple concept. The 3 words are easy to remember, but action is another story. This is evident from the countless enterprises that have failed because people declared victory prematurely, or because they simply did not maintain momentum. Also, don't let the simplicity fool you—the implications and residual effects of this step can be complicated. If the pressure is not kept up on the key players and momentum is lost, significant energy will be needed to rekindle the effort. However, acting too early in the face of an apparent loss of momentum may be perceived as disciplinary and can endanger your credibility. Therefore, the challenge is to maintain a balance between the risks of appearing laissez-faire and those of micromanaging or overreacting.

Symptoms that indicate the effort may be losing momentum include the following:

- Planned changes are delayed.

- Issues identified and marked for action are ignored.

- Key leaders are unavailable for meetings or presentations.

- Recommendations are shelved.

- Decisions are recycled as people have second thoughts.

- Resources, once secured for the project, are committed to other priorities.

If you see any of these signs, your change initiative is likely in trouble. Why do people allow momentum to drop? Why aren't organizations able to just keep it going? There are many reasons.

Exhaustion on the Part of the Leaders

Big surprise: organizational leaders are frequently overcommitted when it comes to corporate initiatives. Therefore, once a few short-term wins are in place, they often scale back on their commitment to the change initiative, simply out of fatigue and necessity. This challenge can be met by rotating guiding team members on and off the team. Such a rotation should involve developing a rotation plan, a clear selection procedure for new members; and an assimilation process for new members through which they learn how the team works.

Failure to See Progress Slowing

As leaders shift their attention to other organizational needs, they often fail to see that progress on the change initiative is slowing. Planning significant milestones along the path to success can help solve this problem. For example, short-term wins can be mapped to an overall progress plan, or a timeline can be developed identifying when significant milestones need to occur. These tools would make a slowdown in progress much easier to spot.

Turnover of Key Change Agents

While rotating team members can prevent loss of momentum, it can also have the opposite effect, by removing key drivers of the change from the project. Therefore, it is critical to recognize when a key driver should stay in place, and also whether new team members are carrying their weight to keep the change effort moving forward.

Flagging Team Morale

Lack of short-term wins or other evidence of success, internal coordination problems, people problems, or any of several other issues can lead to declining morale, a loss of energy, and reduced momentum. Here are some ways to ensure that the level of urgency is sustained:

- Leaders need to publicly reaffirm how the effort is critical to organizational success.

- Converted change resisters should relate why they came around, speak of the progress of the initiative, and discuss their learning as a result.

- Managers should be extra attentive to each sign of progress and give pep talks to individual employees where appropriate.

- Feedback from customers or shareholders that might be motivating should be communicated to those involved in the change.

- Leaders, managers, or employees who are feeling the benefits of the change should describe the new environment they are working in for their colleagues.

Taking Too Long

The mantra "don't let up" is easy if the initiative is relatively small. But if you've got big, long-range changes to make, the challenge becomes much more difficult, if people perceive that the change is taking far too long without making progress. The main way to counteract this key source of lost momentum is to break up long projects into shorter milestones, so that you can declare multiple short-term victories. When you do this, the continual flow of positive communications demonstrates to people that the change is not only progressing but "taking root" as well.

Gauging Effectiveness

Characteristics of Sustained Momentum

Look for the following indicators as evidence that your change team is doing a good job at not letting up:

- Leaders are actively monitoring and measuring the progress of the change.

- New projects and initiatives are launched to make more significant changes to the organization's processes, technology, and systems.

- Other related systems and HR infrastructures continue to be adjusted to fit the vision as it unfolds.

- New change leaders emerge.

- Leaders of the organization are talking about the progress and the successes of the change.

- Based on performance feedback, leaders remain active in clarifying priorities to achieve the desired change.

- Leaders remain emphatic, even passionate, in their determination to see the vision become a reality.

- Time and effort are directed to support managers and employees during the transition.

You can also flip the perspective and use these points—in the negative—to gauge whether you're in danger of losing steam. If progress slows at this stage, it is critical to develop targeted interventions that drive the level of urgency back up and keep the change effort moving forward.

The Don't Let Up Diagnostic

When things seem to be going well, the temptation to relax and sit back can be hard to resist. This is especially true when individuals have been devoting lots of time and effort to the change initiative. However, if you let up too soon, all of the progress that has been made can quickly dissipate and your project will slide down the slippery slope into oblivion. This tool will help you gauge people's perception of leadership and how they are sustaining their efforts to make the change initiative a success.

How to Use the Diagnostic

- Distribute the Don't Let Up Diagnostic (assessment tool 7-2) to individuals whose perspective is desired.

- Ask the individuals being surveyed to answer the questions according to their own experiences and knowledge of the organization.

- As indicated on the directions that accompany the diagnostic, respondents will assign a rating of 1 to 6 to each question, with 1 indicating "strongly disagree" and 6 indicating "strongly agree."

- Tally the results after the sheets have been returned to you. The farther the results are from the maximum score possible, the more pressing the problem.

Suggestions for Improvement

It seems obvious, but for a change effort to be successful, you must keep going until the job is done. If the scores on this diagnostic were low, this indicates that the drive for continuous improvement and realization of the transformation has slowed down, if not stalled completely. The following suggestions may help boost the momentum of your change initiative.

Stay Focused; Don't Get Distracted

After attaining a short-term win or overcoming an unexpected challenge, it is easy to become distracted. When these successes are major milestones, it's easy to fool oneself into thinking that the transformation has been achieved. The reality is, tired people often

The don't let up diagnostic

Instructions

- Please read each statement and indicate the extent to which it describes the norm in your organization as a whole. Your responses should reflect what you have experienced as well as what you have generally observed in your organization.
- Answer the questions using a 6-point scale; the far left of the scale indicates that you strongly disagree and the far right of the scale indicates that you strongly agree. Please respond by checking the box that corresponds most closely to your situation.
- If you do not know the answer, check the "Do not know" box.
- Please take the time to respond to the open-ended questions at the end of the survey. Your responses are crucial in improving the change initiative.
- Be honest in your responses. There are no right or wrong answers, and your answers will remain completely confidential.

Don't let up	Strongly disagree (1)					Strongly agree (6)	Do not know
As a member of this organization, I . . .							
1. Have seen improvements and/or successes as a result of the change effort within the last six months.	☐	☐	☐	☐	☐	☐	☐
2. Believe that leadership recognizes the interdependencies of all the ongoing initiatives that support our transformation.	☐	☐	☐	☐	☐	☐	☐
3. Believe that all of the initiatives are well coordinated.	☐	☐	☐	☐	☐	☐	☐
4. Feel that we're constantly building off our most recent success and pursuing the next big win/major milestone.	☐	☐	☐	☐	☐	☐	☐
5. Feel that our organizational structure, appraisal systems, culture, and so forth, are all coordinated in support of our transformation.	☐	☐	☐	☐	☐	☐	☐
6. Feel that we are capable of moving forward with even greater speed.	☐	☐	☐	☐	☐	☐	☐
7. Feel that we are capable of tackling even bigger initiatives.	☐	☐	☐	☐	☐	☐	☐
8. See that additional people have been brought on board to assist with the transformation.	☐	☐	☐	☐	☐	☐	☐
9. See that the transformation is penetrating the organization.	☐	☐	☐	☐	☐	☐	☐
10. Believe that leadership is doing a good job of continually promoting our transformation and goals for the future.	☐	☐	☐	☐	☐	☐	☐
11. Believe that management does a good job of planning, organizing, and implementing specific changes in support of our transformation.	☐	☐	☐	☐	☐	☐	☐
12. Understand that numerous waves of change are necessary to achieve our transformation.	☐	☐	☐	☐	☐	☐	☐

The don't let up diagnostic *(continued)*

Don't let up	Strongly disagree (1)					Strongly agree (6)	Do not know
13. Believe my organization is committed to making the change a success.	☐	☐	☐	☐	☐	☐	☐
14. Believe my organization is focused on the long-term benefits of the multiple change efforts we have going on.	☐	☐	☐	☐	☐	☐	☐
15. Believe my organization is utilizing resources effectively on multiple change efforts.	☐	☐	☐	☐	☐	☐	☐
Subtotals	x 1	+ x 2	+ x 3	+ x 4	+ x 5	+ x 6	

= Grand total

To get your totals

Add the check marks in vertical columns to get subtotals. Multiply that total by the number at the bottom of each column. Then add the subtotals together to get the grand total.

Grand total: 15 = serious problems, 90 = no problems. Any score below a 60 indicates a need for improvement.

Open-ended feedback

1. What is different now that the change has been implemented, or is it the same old thing with a different label?

_____

_____

_____

_____

_____

2. How do you feel about the changes that have taken place? How have these changes personally affected you?

_____

_____

_____

_____

_____

3. Do you think we have enough momentum to achieve our transformation? If not, how do you suggest we build our momentum?

_____

_____

_____

_____

_____

4. What are leaders doing that make you believe they are really serious about this change effort?

_____

_____

_____

_____

_____

want to declare victory and be done. Thus, they convince themselves that momentum will carry them the rest of the way to the end goal. Don't be seduced. With so many components to a change effort, it is critical to stay focused on *all* that needs to be transformed until the change effort is completely realized. As mentioned earlier, to avoid this dangerous pitfall, leaders must break the change into smaller pieces. Once any sort of win is achieved, successful guiding teams pick the next elements to be tackled and begin the minicycle all over again. They maintain a sense of urgency by communicating stories that keep events in perspective and that take people beyond the euphoria of short-term wins. They add fresh, energetic people to the guiding teams and find new ways to communicate about the transformation.

Consolidate and Coordinate Both Completed and Ongoing Change

Change efforts will branch out into different divisions, plants, initiatives, and levels. Because change efforts involve nonroutine work, it can be quite difficult to coordinate these activities. The lack of coordination drains resources and slows action. To avoid having multiple change initiatives running in parallel, it is essential to consolidate all these efforts into a single program of initiatives. If multiple initiatives already exist, they must be managed in a way that does not send employees mixed messages about the priorities.

Delegate, Purge, and Streamline

Change efforts require a lot of energy, motivation, and hard work. Fatigue—both mental and physical—can easily set in unless you modify your own work habits in concert with the organizational changes. Successful leaders and change drivers manage their workload in the same spirit as the change transformation. In essence, they rethink the way they do their work: they reduce travel time by teleconferencing; they cancel the Tuesday morning meetings that have occurred for the last five decades because they are no longer necessary; they discontinue the six reports they get daily because they don't need them in report format; they purge their calendar of everything that has no current pressing relevance; they delegate down, up, and sideways. Remember, if your organization is reorganizing, why shouldn't you?

Communicating in This Step

Just as you should guard against the dangers of running out of steam, becoming distracted, and declaring premature victory by not letting up, you should not lessen your efforts to communicate progress of the change effort. This communication is almost as integral to sustaining momentum as the progress itself. Here are some specific points of advice for communicating while maintaining urgency in the midst of change:

- *Ensure two-way communication.* Well-designed, high-impact communication processes are needed to support both top-down and bottom-up information flows during this highly disruptive time for the organization.

- *Revise key messages to reflect the new focus and pace of change.* Strike a balance between proclaiming short-term wins and emphasizing the work that remains. Keep the key aspect of the change visible and show progress. Break the initiative into sections and show accomplishments as well as what still needs to be done.

- *Manage simultaneous communication objectives.* The communication effort becomes much more complex when different parts of the organization are in different stages of change. Some people may still need to be made aware of the new vision and its implications for their work, while others need to be motivated to act.

- *Address new stakeholders.* Once the change effort has achieved a certain level of credibility and some of the risks have been eliminated with proven results, share this status with your external stakeholders:

    - ✓ Shareholders
    - ✓ Customers
    - ✓ Community groups
    - ✓ Government institutions
    - ✓ Regulatory bodies
    - ✓ Other subsidiaries

Before delivering this message, however, it is useful to determine what questions to ask these stakeholders and what information you need from them.

- *Reinforce and re-communicate a vision that may have grown stale.* Find new, relevant ways to communicate the overall purpose of the change initiative. The challenge is to revitalize the message while remaining consistent with the vision.

- *Use new channels to communicate to the broader audience and to capture and act on feedback.* At this stage of the process, communication takes on a more consultative nature. While it is still important to communicate broad vision, targets, and concepts, a large part of the communication effort is now devoted to describing how the change will impact each specific group and learning what barriers and concerns they will face.

Checkpoint Before Moving to the Final Step

During this time, employees may experience significant, even radical, changes in the way they go about their work. But how much change is too much? And are your employees coping effectively with the stress? In addition to their new roles and responsibilities, new tools and new expectations are being pressed upon them. The skills and knowledge they have developed over time may no longer be relevant or sufficient to help them when they run into problems. When they turn to their managers for help, they often find that the managers feel just as helpless. As a result, employees become terribly frustrated in their effort to succeed. They may feel stressed, be unmotivated, or even leave the company.

Employees' main complaint during this time is often not the change itself but surviving in an environment where things are changing considerably *all the time*. The pace and amount of change directed at them, combined with high anxiety regarding their future position in the organization, contribute to their stress. The challenge for leaders is to maintain a brisk pace of change while also managing the stress level in the organization. The following suggestions may help you accomplish this goal:

- *Check the pulse—keep a finger on the level of stress in the organization.* This can be accomplished by collecting feedback, either formally through surveys or focus groups or informally through day-to-day conversations. The situation must be detected before it deteriorates to a dangerous level. Once a group is driven to high stress, it is very difficult to drive change, as they will tend to revert to working habits that are familiar to them.

- *Clarify what will change and what will not change.* To be comfortable making more radical change, people need to know what will stay the same. This information gives people a sense of security. Without it, few will take the necessary risks.

- *Provide supporting mechanisms to cope with the change.* Set up chat groups, have managers spend more time listening to their employees, conduct surveys, and so forth.

- *Help people to solve problems and to recognize and manage stress.* Teach employees what they have control over and what resources they have to help them.

Stories to Remember from Step 7 of *The Heart of Change*

Use the following story summaries and questions to help you execute step 7.

"PE Ratios"

When this healthcare company faced the possibility of shutting down, it initiated change by comparing itself to other healthcare companies. When employees started seeing positive results, they were more motivated than ever to meet new challenges. However, once the company was the leader in the field, the workforce became complacent and did not see the need to continue growing. As a result, the firm decided to shift from just comparing itself to other companies, to looking at the company "from the investor's point of view." This forced the company to compare its price to earning (PE) ratios not only to direct competitors, but to companies in the broader healthcare field. Introducing a new external problem helped people see the potential loss of investors and raised the urgency levels of many employees.

(Summarized from *The Heart of Change,* pages 144–146)

- How are you monitoring your progress?

- Do your leaders have the sense of urgency to see this effort through to completion?

- What do you need to do to keep urgency up?

- Do you need new yardsticks to gauge your success?

- Are you really challenging yourself to be the very best you can be?

"The Merchant of Fear"

To address company problems, Phil Nolan and Steve Featherstone created "Action Labs," which are cross-functional teams given a great latitude and authority to address an issue. They created an Action Lab to address the company's poor track record of investment planning. The team members created a video skit using characters such as the Merchant of Fear, the Glory Hunter, and the People Protector to portray the way senior executives behaved during the investment planning process. The video was shared with the top executives, and it made a powerful impact. By highlighting the negative behaviors among the group in a more relaxed environment, the executives were able to see themselves as they were seen by others—something that could never have been done without the open environment created by the Action Lab team.

(Summarized from *The Heart of Change,* pages 147–150)

- What are you doing to encourage people to take risks?

- Are you creating an environment where your people have the time, resources, and encouragement to work on the bigger problems you are facing?

- What have you done to attack the "sturdy silos" and politics in your organization?

- What additional actions must be taken to remove the slack in your performance?

"Reducing Twenty-Five Pages to Two"

After the change teams had been working together for a while, leadership began to hear complaints from team members that they had too much work. To address the concerns, leadership encouraged employees to look at their workload and identify job tasks that might not be necessary. The company began to address the twenty-five-page monthly report and found that most people didn't read it. So, the report was transformed into a two-page version containing agreed-upon financial metrics.   (Summarized from *The Heart of Change,* pages 152–154)

- What work are you doing that could be jettisoned?

- What activities can you simplify?

- What really adds value to your work and what is keeping you from doing it?

- What can be delegated upward, sideways, and downward?

- Will dying help? No. So what will you do to prevent it?

"The Street"

This company had already tackled its customer service goals and achieved a 99 percent rate of on-time, accurate shipments, which quickly turned into complacency. Improving the customer service goals left the company with thousands of unused square feet in the manufacturing facility. When one of the designers approached Jack Jacobs with the idea of transforming the empty space into offices, Jack wanted to reflect upon the idea to see if it would support the vision. Because part of the vision emphasized community, Jack asked a design team to create a plan for reconfiguring the space to support community as well as the change initiative. The team's plan achieved a greater sense of community by putting manufacturing at the center of the plant and increasing the interaction between plant workers, administrative staff, executives, and so on.   (Summarized from *The Heart of Change,* pages 155–157)

- Are there aspects of the vision you still have not tackled?

- What else must you do so that your people see and feel the results of the vision?

- What "streets" should you build?

More Resources

Booth, Lila. "The Change Audit: A New Tool to Monitor Your Biggest Organizational Challenge." **Harvard Management Update,** March 1998.

In this article, Booth presents a tool for monitoring and maintaining momentum in the change process and outlines the crucial steps needed for real change to take hold.

Browne, M. Neil, and Keeley, Stuart M. **Asking the Right Questions: A Guide to Critical Thinking**. Englewood Cliffs, NJ: Prentice Hall, 1997.

Leaders and teams must continuously assess the progress of a change effort in order to uncover obstacles and determine appropriate actions. This work focuses on the critical thinking and questioning skills necessary to collect and assess information in an effective, unbiased way.

Fullan, Michael. **Leading in a Culture of Change**. San Francisco: Jossey-Bass, 2001.

Sustaining momentum and continuing to advance implementation efforts requires skillful leadership. This work outlines a framework of five capacities required for successful leaders of change: moral purpose, understanding change, relationship building, knowledge creation and sharing, and coherence making.

Maurer, Rick. **Beyond the Wall of Resistance: Unconventional Strategies That Build Support for Change**. New York: Bard Press, 1996.

The success of the change and ultimately the organization often depends on how well managers can work with resistance. This book provides a fresh approach that shows why the conventional ways of dealing with resistance—using power, deal making, force of reason, ignoring it—actually increase opposition.

Morgan, Nick. "How to Overcome 'Change Fatigue.'" **Harvard Management Update**, July 2001.

Employee motivation is more important than heroic, all-knowing leaders in making change efforts a success. In this article, panelists at the Burning Questions 2001 conference, David Garvin, Henry Mintzberg, Rosabeth Moss Kanter, and Ricardo Semler, discuss ideas about change.

Pfeffer, Jeffrey, and Sutton, Robert I. **The Knowing-Doing Gap: How Smart Companies Turn Knowledge into Action**. Boston: Harvard Business School Press, 1999.

Action is the key to sustaining long-term change. In this work, the authors present why some companies are better than others at turning knowledge into action.

Ryan, Kathleen, and Oestreich, Daniel K. **Driving Fear Out of the Workplace: Creating the High-Trust, High-Performance Organization**. San Francisco: Jossey-Bass, 1998.

Fear and anxiety severely hinder an organization's ability to initiate and sustain change. This book confronts the fears that permeate today's business environment and shows managers how to address them to increase trust and individual performance.

Whitney, Diana, Cooperrider, David, and Trosten-Bloom, Amanda. **The Power of Appreciative Inquiry: A Practical Guide to Positive Change**. New York: Berrett-Koehler Publishers, 2002.

This book outlines a new approach to organizational change—appreciative inquiry—which improves performance by encouraging people to study, discuss, learn from, and build on what is working, rather than simply trying to fix what is not.

Make It Stick

Tradition is a powerful force. Leaps into the future can slide back into the past. We keep a change in place by helping to create a new, supportive, and sufficiently strong organizational culture. A supportive culture provides roots for the new ways of operating. It keeps the revolutionary technology, the globalized organization, the innovative strategy, or the more efficient processes working to make you a winner.

—from Step 8 of *The Heart of Change*

Purpose

Once you've had some key short-term wins, gained good momentum, and have actually shifted people's behaviors to fit the change vision, these new behaviors need to be truly woven into the fabric of the organization. If your organizational transformation is not properly supported and reinforced by a vital organizational culture, the effort needed to maintain the desired outcome will continue to seem like extra effort, and will become too difficult to sustain. In order to achieve lasting integration of the change, leaders must model the new behavior themselves, and reward and recognize others who also demonstrate the new behavior. This will enable the changes to take root and a new corporate culture to emerge.

Approach

To make change last, new behaviors need to become a part of the formal and informal systems, practices, and habits that form the organization's culture. The key elements that make new behaviors stick involve:

1. Achieving tangible results as quickly as possible.

2. Showing *how* the change is working, and *why* the old ways won't work.

3. Measuring and supporting the sustained performance.

4. Ensuring that leadership will support and model the new behaviors.

5. Initiating necessary turnover.

Following are some of the key areas to consider when focusing on how to make the new behaviors stick:

- Management systems
  - ✓ Structures, roles, and responsibilities
  - ✓ Goals and performance
  - ✓ Information systems
  - ✓ Management processes

- Organizational infrastructures
  - ✓ Recruiting and hiring processes
  - ✓ Orientation, education, and training
  - ✓ Goal setting
  - ✓ Performance appraisals
  - ✓ Reward and recognition systems
  - ✓ Career development and promotion
  - ✓ Communication processes

- Informal practices
  - ✓ Coaching and mentoring
  - ✓ Social gatherings
  - ✓ Informal recognition
  - ✓ Networks
  - ✓ Clubs

Achieving Tangible Results Quickly

As you can see, this aspect of step 8 is closely related to step 6, create short-term wins. It is crucial that the new behaviors achieve tangible, desired results for a sustained period of time during (and after) the change initiative. Positive results make it very clear that the new practices work and that they are preferable to old habits. These results may come in the form of short-term wins, such as a rise in customer retention, a decrease in service calls, or a more efficient method for sharing customer information; or they could be longer-term payoffs, such as a rise in recognized performance rankings or customer rankings, a more positive and energized atmosphere in the organization, or a renewed creativity and entrepreneurial spirit among employees.

Showing *How* the Change Is Working, and *Why* the Old Ways Won't Work

People need to witness and understand the connection between new practices and performance improvement before they will admit the validity of the changes and feel secure enough to experiment with and adopt them. You need to clearly show all involved in the change effort just how their new behaviors and practices are leading to improved results. Just as important, they need to understand how the behavior in the old culture was formed and why it will no longer work in the new culture, so that the powerful pull and inertia of tradition—the way things were—is kept to a minimum.

Measuring and Supporting Sustained Performance

To make change last, the management systems, leaders, and organizational infrastructure need to develop, reinforce, measure, and reward the new behaviors.

This process began in previous steps:

- Step 5 (enable action): Change the systems and infrastructure to remove significant and immediate barriers to the change.

- Step 6 (create short-term wins): Demonstrate that progress is being achieved in a visible, meaningful, and timely manner.

- Step 7 (don't let up): Broaden the effort to change interdependent systems and structures that do not fit the vision.

This step entails following up to ensure that the changes to the organizational systems are working as intended as well as highlighting examples of how the change is taking effect. Moreover, sharing stories of individuals who are demonstrating the new behaviors and the success they are having will get others to see the positive effects and help weave the change into the fabric of the organization.

Developing Means to Ensure Leadership Support

If the change effort is to last, the ongoing leadership development and succession process needs to select and promote leaders who will model and support the new behaviors. Future leaders should have enthusiasm for the new practices and values that are compatible with the vision, as well as any specialized skills or experience it requires. To ensure that new leaders are aligned with the evolving organization, it is important to consider the following questions:

- What criteria are used to select and promote new leaders?

- How are corporate values communicated to new leaders?

- What behaviors by new leaders will and will not be recognized and reinforced?

- What opportunities are given to new leaders to develop and demonstrate these behaviors?

If leaders are not selected carefully, retaining them may be challenging, since groups tend to reject those with different values. Bringing in a new leader whose values or perspective is significantly out of alignment with those he will be leading can be disastrous. To enhance the success of new leaders, consider these questions:

- What level of coaching do new leaders get?

- What type of support can they expect from their peers?

- What informal activities, gatherings, networks, or habits are perpetuated that may keep out new individuals or those with different beliefs?

- Are decisions made in situations that are inaccessible to new leaders?

Initiating Necessary Turnover

By definition, a transformation requires people to change their behavior. Not all individuals will be able to make the change—that's only human. Individuals who cannot or will not change should be afforded a reasonable opportunity to turn their performance around. A performance improvement plan that identifies the problem, expectations, and a date for resolution is an important first step. In addition, if knowledge, skills, or ability is an issue, be sure that training and development opportunities are suggested and made available. If these efforts still fail, it is important to show your compassion and respect for your people by offering meaningful alternatives to those who cannot perform effectively in the new organization. If there is no reasonable alternative within the organization, offer outplacement assistance so that individuals have some support while seeking other employment.

Outcomes

When the change is "sticking," more than likely you'll know it and feel it. If you're effectively using the eight steps and your change effort is truly being absorbed, you'll witness the following:

- An organization that selects, develops, and promotes the leaders who model, encourage, and support the desired behaviors.

- An organization that has embedded the changed behaviors so thoroughly into its operating style that a new culture has emerged.

- An organizational infrastructure that develops and reinforces the correct practices and behaviors within the workforce.

- A workforce that has the capability and motivation to achieve and sustain the desired results and that has enhanced its ability to manage change effectively.

- Management systems that measure and reward the desired outcomes.

Key Implementation Challenges

Making change stick is the classic challenge associated with organizational transformation efforts. Probably anyone reading this has been involved with change initiatives that had some early success, but then could not be sustained. Making change stick is difficult for many reasons. The challenges described next are likely to emerge during any significant change effort. The key to meeting each of them is having an aligned set of guiding teams that can handle issues as they come up in a manner that is consistent with the change vision.

Culture Resists Change

Corporate culture consists of two main elements:

- *Norms of behavior:* Behavioral norms define the ways in which people are expected to act in the organization. They persist because people teach these practices to new employees, both explicitly and through modeling of behavior, accepting and rewarding those who fit in and ostracizing those who do not.

- *Values:* Culture also reflects the values of the people in the organization. These values persist because organizations tend to attract and retain individuals who share the same beliefs, and criticize and reject those who do not.

Therefore, the culture of an organization can stymie any transformation efforts that go against the established norms of behavior, attitudes, and values. To overcome this challenge, leadership must get management and employees to see the benefits that will be derived once the change has been woven into the day-to-day operations of the organization.

Culture Change Comes Last

Leaders often identify the organizational culture as a key obstacle to a change initiative. Although the groundwork for a change in culture is laid early in the transformation process, the changes cannot be firmly entrenched until the "new" behavior is no longer seen as "new" but rather as "the way we do things around here." People need to practice the new behaviors for a period of time before they can become ingrained. Therefore, organizations can find themselves in a bit of a catch-22: it is difficult to adopt the new behaviors until the culture has changed, but the culture is not likely to change until the new behaviors have been adopted. Organizations can manage this particular challenge by having leaders at multiple levels model the new behaviors as well as reward and recognize others who do so. Key to this strategy is not overreacting when an employee tries to behave in accordance with the change initiative but stumbles. It is at this point that all eyes are on leaders to see how they respond.

Gauging Effectiveness

Indicators That a Change Is Sticking

The behaviors shown in table 8-1 indicate whether the organization is adopting the change. Some of the indicators (at the beginning of the list) may be seen early in the change process; others (toward the end of the list) will be witnessed only after some time, in some cases as long as three to five years. In addition, be creative in looking at specific areas across the organization for new ways to ensure the new behavior becomes the norm.

Inevitably, some individuals will hold on to the old behaviors and habits. A culture change *will* happen, however, when a critical mass of employees exhibit the new behaviors consistently, over an extended period of time, and see that this has become the "way things get done around here."

The Make It Stick Diagnostic

As we've discussed, for new behaviors to stick, leaders throughout the organization must model those behaviors as well as reward and recognize others who demonstrate the behavior. This tool helps determine the extent to which the new behavior is sticking and, as a result, the probability that the new culture will emerge.

To use the diagnostic successfully, follow these steps:

- Distribute the Make It Stick Diagnostic (assessment tool 8-1) to individuals whose perspective is desired.

TABLE 8-1

Making it stick effectiveness checklist

Indicators of a behavioral shift	Indicators that behavior is not changing
Change leaders are sought for advice and input.	Change leaders are criticized.
Results of the changes are used to evaluate how best to continue or improve.	Benefits of the change are challenged, questioned, or discounted.
Emphasis is on what needs to be adjusted, revised, or improved.	Emphasis is on what can be maintained or kept.
Focus is on successes and learning.	Focus is on the costs and sacrifices.
More decisions are made consistent with the vision and the marketplace.	More decisions are made consistent with historical successes and past practices.
Old behaviors and traditions are used to describe how things have changed.	Old behaviors and traditions are used to rationalize mistakes and justify new decisions.
People seek to understand what they need to do and what is expected of them to be successful in the new environment.	People act consistently with the way they (or others) have been successful in the past.
Change leaders and promoters gain more influence.	Change resisters get more and more time and attention.
Change leaders and promoters are finding support and resources for more changes.	Change leaders become increasingly frustrated.
People with high tenure begin to leave the organization or subunit because they acknowledge they don't fit in anymore.	Recently hired people leave the organization because they don't fit in or are frustrated in their efforts.

- Ask the individuals being surveyed to answer the questions according to their own experiences and knowledge of the organization.

- As indicated on the directions that accompany the diagnostic, respondents will assign a rating of 1 to 6 to each question, with 1 indicating "strongly disagree" and 6 indicating "strongly agree."

- Tally the results after the sheets have been returned to you. The farther the results are from the maximum score possible, the more pressing the problem.

ASSESSMENT TOOL 8-1

The make it stick diagnostic

Instructions

- Please read each statement and indicate the extent to which it describes the norm in your organization as a whole. Your responses should reflect what you have experienced as well as what you have generally observed in your organization.
- Answer the questions using a 6-point scale; the far left of the scale indicates that you strongly disagree and the far right of the scale indicates that you strongly agree. Please respond by checking the box that corresponds most closely to your situation.
- If you do not know the answer, check the "Do not know" box.
- Please take the time to respond to the open-ended questions at the end of the survey. Your responses are crucial in improving the change initiative.
- Be honest in your responses. There are no right or wrong answers, and your answers will remain completely confidential.

Making change stick	Strongly disagree (1)					Strongly agree (6)	Do not know
As a member of this organization, I . . .							
1. Believe that the new behaviors will stay, even if key leaders involved in the effort leave.	☐	☐	☐	☐	☐	☐	☐
2. Agree that leadership spends a lot of time promoting new attitudes and behaviors.	☐	☐	☐	☐	☐	☐	☐
3. Feel that leadership takes the time to explain why the way we did things in the past is no longer suited to our future goals.	☐	☐	☐	☐	☐	☐	☐
4. Believe that new practices resulting from the change effort are superior to old ones.	☐	☐	☐	☐	☐	☐	☐
5. Agree that people who behave/perform in ways that support our new vision are rewarded.	☐	☐	☐	☐	☐	☐	☐
6. Believe that leadership succession is carefully planned. Executives with yesterday's mentality will not be placed in key leadership positions.	☐	☐	☐	☐	☐	☐	☐
7. See that new, forward-thinking leaders have been hired.	☐	☐	☐	☐	☐	☐	☐
8. Agree that the organization is careful in whom they hire. New people will not be brought on board if they exhibit traits of a culture that we are trying to move away from.	☐	☐	☐	☐	☐	☐	☐
9. See leadership exhibiting new behaviors.	☐	☐	☐	☐	☐	☐	☐
10. See management/supervisors exhibiting new behaviors.	☐	☐	☐	☐	☐	☐	☐
11. See my peers exhibiting new behaviors.	☐	☐	☐	☐	☐	☐	☐
12. Agree that we are consistently rewarded for behavior that suits the new way of doing things.	☐	☐	☐	☐	☐	☐	☐
13. See leaders consistently reinforcing the vision.	☐	☐	☐	☐	☐	☐	☐
14. Feel that traditions are not holding us back from behaving according to the new vision.	☐	☐	☐	☐	☐	☐	☐

The make it stick diagnostic *(continued)*

Making change stick	Strongly disagree (1)					Strongly agree (6)	Do not know
15. See new behavior becoming a part of the way we operate.	☐	☐	☐	☐	☐	☐	☐
Subtotals	x 1	+ x 2	+ x 3	+ x 4	+ x 5	+ x 6	
= Grand total							

To get your totals

Add the check marks in vertical columns to get subtotals. Multiply that total by the number at the bottom of each column. Then add the subtotals together to get the grand total.

Grand total: 15 = serious problems, 90 = no problems. Any score below a 60 indicates a need for improvement.

Open-ended feedback

1. What additional things can be done to make the change initiative stick?

_____
_____
_____
_____
_____

2. Do you feel that the organization truly supports the change effort? What evidence do you have?

_____
_____
_____
_____
_____

3. What new behaviors do you see leaders and employees exhibiting on a daily basis?

_____
_____
_____
_____
_____

4. How are employees who exhibit new behaviors consistent with the change effort recognized and/or rewarded?

_____
_____
_____
_____
_____

Suggestions for Improvement

Creating an environment where change will stick involves creating new habits, behaviors, and traditions. This may be the hardest step in the change process because it requires breaking away from traditional, entrenched behaviors both during and after the change has been implemented. If your respondents scored low in this area, you have probably stopped the change effort one step too soon—employees are not exhibiting the behavior needed to make the change stick. The following suggestions may help ensure that your hard-earned changes endure.

Don't Equate Behavioral Change with Cultural Change

We often act as if we believe that any change in a group's behavior means a change in their culture. Don't confuse culture with an influential boss, a compensation system, or even a group habit. Culture has deeper roots than rational thought, so when an individual or group tries something new, even if it makes powerful sense, the organization nudges the individual back to the norm. A change in a group's behavior becomes part of the new culture only when the behavior becomes ingrained. Without constant attention and reinforcement from guiding teams or a performance-reward system, the behavior will not stick over the long haul.

Hire the Right People

Getting succession right is crucial, especially when replacing a member of a guiding team. Make sure the successor understands the importance and value of the change, behaves appropriately, and understands where the team stands in the progress toward change. Also, keep in mind that, due to the power and visibility of the positions, promotions are important in solidifying the new culture. When there is rapid growth, you need to hire and promote people who not only mesh well with the new way of doing things, but who *embody* these new ways. Be aware that hiring many new people in a short period of time requires extra awareness and effort to acculturate the new employees. In addition, a large influx of new leaders could either help you build a new culture quickly (since the new employees are not part of the old culture) or create huge problems (because they didn't go through the initial change effort and don't understand the value of the vision and the norms).

Be Patient and Persistent

First, realize that culture cannot be changed overnight. Breaking old habits and embracing new values are difficult, especially if your organization dates back a few decades or more. Be patient. Persistence is the key to success. Often, people feel satisfied with the change effort and do not build the roots that will make the change stick. Their efforts will be wasted when people revert to their old habits. Make sure all the key leaders know what the winning behaviors are, the actions that need to be sustained, how they will model the new behaviors, and the need to recognize others for exhibiting the new behavior. Eventually, through such relentless efforts, the vision will sink in and the old ways will be replaced by the new culture.

Communicating in This Step

At this stage of the change process, many changes have been implemented. People are focused on getting along in the new environment and solving problems as they arise. They are trying to establish a new routine and a sense of stability in this new reality.

Thus, communication efforts should focus on showing how the vision is working and embedding the new behaviors and practices as norms in the organizational culture. These efforts should emphasize the following actions:

- Broadly publicizing the results and benefits of the change.

- Recognizing and celebrating achievements and personal contributions.

- Linking organizational successes to the change initiative.

- Acknowledging how the old culture served the company but is no longer appropriate.

- Educating employees on how the new/modified values serve as the foundation for continued success.

- Promoting role models that embody the new behaviors and values.

- Reinforcing the need to continuously change, and where to focus effort.

- Maintaining dialogue among leaders, managers, and employees about challenges arising in the new work environment, the solutions found, and the adjustments needed.

- Seeking feedback when the benefits of this change are questioned or misunderstood, or when changes are criticized.

Stories to Remember from Step 8 of *The Heart of Change*

Use the following story summaries and questions to help you weave the new behavior into the fabric of the organization.

"The Boss Went to Switzerland"

John Harris's division successfully eliminated excess layers of management and supervision, enabling them to react more quickly to challenges. Other leaders in the company would challenge the minimal structure, arguing that growing areas needed more supervision to pre-vent mistakes or that they needed to create management opportunities for promising employees. However, John stuck to his plan, which gave empowerment and accountability to front-line employees. When John was transferred to Switzerland, his former division's results collapsed in just three years, so John was sent to work with his old division and get them back on track. John found that his replacement did not share his vision for a lean organization structure and had added multiple layers. As John began working with the division again to remove the layers of man-agement, increase accountability, and empower his staff, he realized how critical it was for others to share his vision in order to sustain the results.   (Summarized from *The Heart of Change,* pages 162–164)

- What should you be doing to ensure that the intended behavior is sticking?

- Does your governance model reinforce the principles of your vision?

- What are you doing to keep old behavior from creeping back?

- Are your guiding teams modeling the new behavior and reinforc-ing/recognizing others?

"The Path to the Patient"

The researchers and developers in this pharmaceutical company viewed themselves as successful in contributing to the launch of new drugs into the market. However, they learned that because they had operated in silos, it was costing them 50 percent more than necessary for each launch and taking twice as long. They began a change initiative to achieve their new vision of creating value from research and develop-ment, which resulted in significant improvement. Their biggest challenge was making this new culture stick as new employees entered the com-pany. To bring new employees on board, they created "The Path to the Patient" video, which demonstrated their collaborative process begin-ning with the CEO and ending with messages from patients helped by the drugs. This video *was a powerful way to ingrain the vision into the culture.*   (Summarized from *The Heart of Change,* pages 166–169)

- What are you doing to ensure that your new employees see and feel the behavior you really want?

- Do your people really see and feel the results of their efforts?

- What are your guiding teams doing to communicate the vision so that it is seen and felt?

"Promoting the Thirty-Something"

This newspaper underwent significant change in a six-year period, expanding from a regionally based newspaper to a national one. While there were several logical candidates for the new head of planning, they did not always support the new culture by following the company's "Rules of the Road." Denise Warren, a woman in her thirties who was on a flexible work schedule, was selected for the position instead because she had consistently lived the Rules of the Road while also achieving results. By carefully considering the individuals who are right for the open jobs, this newspaper has found a way to stay on track.

(Summarized from *The Heart of Change,* pages 171–172)

- Are you promoting the right people?

- What bold steps do you still need to take to demonstrate your conviction about the new way of doing things?

- What can you do to put the spotlight on individuals who exemplify the new behaviors?

"The Home Mortgage"

This financial company found a way to involve all employees in reevaluating corporate values by creating something called a "Visionquest." During a Visionquest, all 40,000 employees are linked via satellite, and stories are told that reinforce their values. To demonstrate the value of fairness, one bank executive told a powerful story about how he had allowed a retired couple, virtually ruined by the stock market crash of 1987, to stay in their home. By revisiting stories of their past, they helped to solidify their culture.

(Summarized from *The Heart of Change,* pages 173–175)

- What stories are you sharing regularly that demonstrate your way of doing things?

- How are you using emotion to energize your change effort?

- How do you get your people to see what you care about, and more important, to feel the same way?

- How do you make your new behavior a self-reinforcing process?

More Resources

Beer, Michael, and Nohria, Nitin. **Breaking the Code of Change**. Boston: Harvard Business School Press, 2000.

> This book presents a series of articles that address various change issues, from motivation and leadership to compensation issues to developing lasting organizational change.

Flannery, Thomas P., Hofrichter, David A., and Platten, Paul E. **People, Performance and Pay**. New York: Simon & Schuster, 2002.

> In this book, the authors point out that the pay philosophies of most businesses require radical updates to more closely align with the most common organizational work cultures.

Gibson, Elizabeth, and Billings, Andrew. **Big Change at Best Buy: Working Through Hypergrowth to Sustained Excellence**. Palo Alto, CA: Consulting Psychologists Press, 2003.

> In this book a companywide transformational change at Best Buy is evaluated. The authors outline the proven methods and tools used to help Best Buy achieve its success, including a new tool, the Change Scorecard.

Huselid, Mark A., Ulrich, David, and Becker, Brian. **The HR Scorecard: Linking People, Strategy, and Performance**. Boston: Harvard Business School Press, 2001.

> This book argues that HR needs to shift emphasis from administration to becoming a vital partner in achieving business strategy. Each element of the HR system should

be designed to enhance performance, maximize the quality of human capital, and reinforce the right behaviors across the workforce.

Kotter, John P., and Heskett, James L. **Corporate Culture and Performance**. New York: Simon & Schuster, 1992.

The authors of this comprehensive and critical analysis of corporate culture—the shared beliefs, attitudes, and practices of a company's managers and employees—show how the unwritten rules of a company can profoundly enhance economic performance or, conversely, lead to failure to adapt to changing markets and environments.

Kouzes, James M., and Posner, Barry Z. **Encouraging the Heart: A Leader's Guide to Rewarding and Recognizing Others**. New York: Simon & Schuster, 1997.

To properly embed change into the organization, leaders must encourage and reinforce the right set of behaviors in their employees. This work discusses the principle of "encouraging the heart," which includes building self-confidence through high expectations, connecting performance and rewards, and making people feel like heroes.

Schein, Edgar H. **Organizational Culture and Leadership**. San Francisco: Jossey-Bass, 1996.

In this work, the author focuses on the complex business realities of the '90s and updates his influential understanding of culture. Leaders play a crucial role in successfully applying the principles of culture to achieve their organization's goals.

Rappaport, Alfred, Kohn, Alfie, Hall, Brian, Zehnder, Egon, and Nicoson, Robert D. **Harvard Business Review on Compensation**. Boston: Harvard Business School Publishing, 2001.

This collection presents the pros and cons of different compensation plans and discusses a variety of compensation-related issues, such as making salaries public, stock options, executive compensation, and incentive plans.

Vollman, Thomas E. **The Transformation Imperative: Achieving Market Dominance Through Radical Change**. Boston: Harvard Business School Press, 1996.

Change programs must be deep and fully integrated across the organization for real transformation to take place. The author presents useful tools and a practical framework for analyzing, implementing, and measuring change programs.

The Final Module— Change Readiness

Purpose

Is your organization ready for change? What are the key issues that you will face in phase I, when you are creating a climate for change and need sufficient energy to overcome resistance in the form of fear, anger, or complacency? Or during phase II, engaging the organization, when you need to consider whether leadership is actively engaging stakeholders. Or in phase III, as you implement and sustain change and wonder if it will stick? The affirmative answer to these questions is critically important if you are to realize the benefits from the change. In fact, it is so primary, and obvious, it may seem strange or illogical to put this chapter at the end of this guide rather than at the start. However, until you understand the concepts and approaches behind the eight steps, until you can see the inner workings of these steps and their impact on change, the approach of assessing the organization's readiness for change cannot be fully grasped. Now that we have gone through the eight steps (or, if you are familiar with the eight steps and have decided to turn directly to this chapter), it is time to show why and how you should assess your organization's readiness for change.

Approach

Here are the four basic elements of change readiness assessment and the guiding principles behind them:

1. *Take the temperature: You cannot start real change without a realistic picture of the internal climate of the organization.* Information about the inner state of the organization must be gathered from many sources and from varying levels, so that it is clear and persuasive when presented to the organization's formal and informal leaders. The change readiness assessment offers an objective and comprehensive picture to the people who may be set in their thinking and may not understand the real situation. In other words, instead of having to say, "Our assessment is that . . ." you can say, "All of you have told us that. . . ."

2. *Identify the hurdles: Cultural barriers to change should be identified and addressed early in the change process.* The earlier cultural barriers are identified, the better the chance of getting to root causes and removing or avoiding obstacles. The cost of attacking an issue head-on is always lower than dealing with it later.

3. *Talk to the people in the trenches: The rank and file often know more than their bosses about real needs, real problems, and the potential solutions because they live and breathe them every day.* Encourage upward pressure for change by making top leadership aware of what employees think, feel, do, and want to do. Leaders may need this "informational push" before they can do what is needed to create real change.

4. *Be prepared for push-back: Resistance to change is natural and inevitable.* Make plans to overcome fear, anger, and complacency since they feed resistance. An effective plan to overcome resistance and raise the level of energy begins with

obtaining a realistic picture of the internal sources of resistance and why they exist. Take each source seriously.

Understanding employee, management, and leadership perceptions of any change effort is crucial, since to a significant extent perception is reality. A powerful change readiness assessment uncovers and validates these perceptions and provides the information needed to resolve any issues you uncover. How you overcome a barrier or deal with an issue will depend on whether it is factual, a misperception, or something else.

To this end, a change readiness assessment allows you to gauge your organization's current environment with regard to the most immediate threats associated with change across all eight steps of the change process. You should use this assessment throughout the change process as it will shed light on the areas that threaten your success. Once identified, these potential threats can be proactively defused so they do not become barriers as the change progresses.

When assessing change readiness, consider carefully where you are in the change process. For example, if you are just getting under way, naturally your approach should focus on the steps in the first phase of the change process—creating a climate for change. As you move further into the change effort, you should include the steps in the second and third phases of the change process. It is important to remember that as your change effort progresses, you still want to get temperature readings on the initial steps as they are critical to determining the level of energy being devoted to the change effort. Finally, customize the assessment to meet your needs. Review the items for relevance to insure they properly align with your change effort and modify, delete, or add items to best fit your needs.

Assessment tool 9-1, the Change Readiness Assessment, covers all eight steps of the change process and will help you gauge the most immediate risks associated with change given your firm's current environment. Give careful thought to developing open-ended questions relevant to your particular change effort in order to encourage a rich dialogue during focus group discussion. Using several parts of

The change readiness assessment

Instructions

- Please read each statement and indicate the extent to which it describes the norm in your organization as a whole. Your responses should reflect what you have experienced as well as what you have generally observed in your organization.
- Answer the questions using a 6-point scale; the far left of the scale indicates that you strongly disagree and the far right of the scale indicates that you strongly agree. Please respond by checking the box that corresponds most closely to your situation.
- If you do not know the answer, check the "Do not know" box.
- Be honest in your responses. There are no right or wrong answers, and your answers will remain completely confidential.

Sample demographics

Stakeholder group:	☐ Executive/sponsor	☐ Professional	
	☐ Management	☐ Change initiative team	
	☐ Operations	☐ Other	
Function:	☐ Finance	☐ Marketing	
	☐ IT	☐ Administration	
	☐ Human resources	☐ Other (specify) _____	
	☐ Operations		
Number of years of service:	☐ Less than 1 year	☐ 11–20 years	
	☐ 1–5 years	☐ 21 years or more	
	☐ 6–10 years		
Gender:	☐ Male	☐ Female	

Step 1 Establish a sense of urgency	Strongly disagree (1)					Strongly agree (6)	Do not know
Individuals are asking challenging questions and validating for themselves the need to change.	☐	☐	☐	☐	☐	☐	☐
There is a sense that people have a greater awareness of the competition, the industry and the external environment.	☐	☐	☐	☐	☐	☐	☐
There is a general feeling that we cannot afford to fall short of meeting the objectives of the [name of the change initiative].	☐	☐	☐	☐	☐	☐	☐
More energy and effort is being directed toward meeting the objectives of the [name of the change initiative].	☐	☐	☐	☐	☐	☐	☐
= Total	x 1	+ x 2	+ x 3	+ x 4	+ x 5	+ x 6	

Add vertical columns to get subtotals. Then add the subtotals to get your grand total: 4 = high risk, 24 = low risk. Any score below a 16 is considered a risk.

The change readiness assessment *(continued)*

Step 2 **Build guiding teams**	Strongly disagree (1)					Strongly agree (6)	Do not know
Leadership consistently provides the resources, information and support needed to move [name of change initiative] forward.	☐	☐	☐	☐	☐	☐	☐
Leadership motivates and inspires others to participate in the change effort.	☐	☐	☐	☐	☐	☐	☐
Leadership maintains a consistent approach and direction.	☐	☐	☐	☐	☐	☐	☐
Leadership holds itself accountable for results.	☐	☐	☐	☐	☐	☐	☐
= Total	x 1	+ x 2	+ x 3	+ x 4	+ x 5	+ x 6	

Add vertical columns to get subtotals. Then add the subtotals to get your grand total: 4 = high risk, 24 = low risk. Any score below a 16 is considered a risk.

Step 3 **Get the vision right**	Strongly disagree (1)					Strongly agree (6)	Do not know
Leadership can clearly articulate the change vision.	☐	☐	☐	☐	☐	☐	☐
Our change vision is compelling and desirable.	☐	☐	☐	☐	☐	☐	☐
Most people who will be affected by the change can articulate the vision in three minutes or less.	☐	☐	☐	☐	☐	☐	☐
The vision appeals to the long-term interest of everyone in the organization.	☐	☐	☐	☐	☐	☐	☐
= Total	x 1	+ x 2	+ x 3	+ x 4	+ x 5	+ x 6	

Add vertical columns to get subtotals. Then add the subtotals to get your grand total: 4 = high risk, 24 = low risk. Any score below a 16 is considered a risk.

Step 4 **Communicate for buy-in**	Strongly disagree (1)					Strongly agree (6)	Do not know
We provide timely communication about the change effort.	☐	☐	☐	☐	☐	☐	☐
We keep communication about the change simple, candid, and heartfelt.	☐	☐	☐	☐	☐	☐	☐
We discuss the vision, goals, and strategies of the change in routine management meetings as well as in formal and informal gatherings.	☐	☐	☐	☐	☐	☐	☐
Progress of the change gets conveyed to all levels of the organization in a timely manner.	☐	☐	☐	☐	☐	☐	☐
= Total	x 1	+ x 2	+ x 3	+ x 4	+ x 5	+ x 6	

Add vertical columns to get subtotals. Then add the subtotals to get your grand total: 4 = high risk, 24 = low risk. Any score below a 16 is considered a risk.

ASSESSMENT TOOL 9-1

The change readiness assessment *(continued)*

Step 5 **Enable action**	Strongly disagree (1)					Strongly agree (6)	Do not know
We use recognition and reward systems that inspire, promote optimism, and build self-confidence.	☐	☐	☐	☐	☐	☐	☐
Leaders at all levels actively try to remove barriers that keep people from behaving in accordance with the vision.	☐	☐	☐	☐	☐	☐	☐
Individuals are able to take the action needed to do their jobs effectively without having to involve management in every situation.	☐☐	☐☐	☐☐	☐☐	☐☐	☐☐	☐☐
Managers/supervisors who are unwilling to support change and have the power to inhibit others from doing so are dealt with in an appropriate manner.	☐☐	☐☐	☐☐	☐☐	☐☐	☐☐	☐☐
= Total	x 1	+ x 2	+ x 3	+ x 4	+ x 5	+ x 6	

Add vertical columns to get subtotals. Then add the subtotals to get your grand total: 4 = high risk, 24 = low risk. Any score below a 16 is considered a risk.

Step 6 **Create short-term wins**	Strongly disagree (1)					Strongly agree (6)	Do not know
Quick results are made visible to all.	☐	☐	☐	☐	☐	☐	☐
Leaders at all levels use the results from short-term wins to demonstrate progress.	☐	☐	☐	☐	☐	☐	☐
We regularly recognize and celebrate achievements.	☐	☐	☐	☐	☐	☐	☐
Short-term wins are made visible to everyone.	☐	☐	☐	☐	☐	☐	☐
= Total	x 1	+ x 2	+ x 3	+ x 4	+ x 5	+ x 6	

Add vertical columns to get subtotals. Then add the subtotals to get your grand total: 4 = high risk, 24 = low risk. Any score below a 16 is considered a risk.

the tool in combination with each other provides a clear picture of how people see and feel about the change in the steps you are focusing on. When used in this manner, the initial assessment determines your baseline and thus enables you to evaluate your progress when you conduct future assessments.

ASSESSMENT TOOL 9-1

The change readiness assessment *(continued)*

Step 7 **Don't let up**	Strongly disagree (1)					Strongly agree (6)	Do not know
Leadership clearly monitors and measures the progress of change efforts.	☐	☐	☐	☐	☐	☐	☐
Leadership brings additional resources on board to ensure the success of change efforts.	☐	☐	☐	☐	☐	☐	☐
Leaders seek to use new situations opportunistically to further the change effort.	☐	☐	☐	☐	☐	☐	☐
Leadership does not declare premature victories.	☐	☐	☐	☐	☐	☐	☐
= Total	x 1	+ x 2	+ x 3	+ x 4	+ x 5	+ x 6	

Add vertical columns to get subtotals. Then add the subtotals to get your grand total: 4 = high risk, 24 = low risk. Any score below a 16 is considered a risk.

Step 8 **Make it stick**	Strongly disagree (1)					Strongly agree (6)	Do not know
Leadership rewards and recognizes people whose behavior supports the change vision.	☐	☐	☐	☐	☐	☐	☐
Leaders consistently model the new behavior in support of the vision.	☐	☐	☐	☐	☐	☐	☐
Leadership is willing to let go of individuals who will not support the future of our organization.	☐	☐	☐	☐	☐	☐	☐
Clear performance measures have been created so that employees know when they are demonstrating the "right stuff."	☐	☐	☐	☐	☐	☐	☐
= Total	x 1	+ x 2	+ x 3	+ x 4	+ x 5	+ x 6	

Add vertical columns to get subtotals. Then add the subtotals to get your grand total: 4 = high risk, 24 = low risk. Any score below a 16 is considered a risk.

As noted, the Change Readiness Assessment is usually conducted at the beginning of a project; however, it is not designed for one-time use. Instead, it should be used regularly throughout the change effort to monitor progress, measure existing threats, identify new threats, and develop action plans to reduce these threats while maintaining momentum. The assessment can also be customized to get a "risk reading" at certain critical stages that can help determine what action is needed immediately. For example, if the guiding teams have not observed positive signs that the workforce feels enabled, they can tailor the assessment to determine if the readiness issues are related solely to enablement or if they also encompass low urgency, lack of leadership involvement, and/or a lack of a clear and sustaining vision.

Outcomes

Following are some of the benefits of using the Change Readiness Assessment:

- Leadership gains clear and detailed information about the organization's readiness and capacity to succeed in major change initiatives.

- The organization acquires baseline information for customizing its approach to the proposed change effort, its communication, and its roll-out strategy.

- The organization can identify and focus on internal challenges anticipated in implementing the change initiative.

- Action steps required to ensure project success are laid out.

- People across the organization are given the opportunity to offer their perceptions of the organization's strengths and weaknesses in managing and preparing for change, and to define what they feel is needed for greater effectiveness.

- Issues, resistance, and opportunities are identified and inform the entire change process.

- Leaders, managers, and employees see the gaps between the way things are and the way things must be in order to sustain real change.

Key Challenges

The following challenges frequently emerge when assessing your organization's readiness for a change initiative. Be aware of these possible responses and be ready to stress to the organization the value of the readiness assessment and resulting information. The best way to increase your organization's chances of success in effecting change is doing due diligence and adequate preparation. Plunging in before the organization is ready could very well be disastrous.

Fear of Over Surveying

Many organizations hesitate to administer surveys for fear of over surveying their employees, which can lead to cynicism and jadedness. But be careful not to allow the "over surveying" excuse as a cover for simply resisting assessment for fear of what might be revealed. In this instance, have the senior guiding team complete the survey so that they can see the issues more clearly and be a part of the solution. If you hit a brick wall, try using the survey in a focus group setting where the items are discussed and action steps are developed to overcome the issues that arise during the session. If after trying several different approaches you still have little or no success in gauging organizational readiness, it may be time to tell leadership candidly that they are headed for failure if reliable feedback cannot be obtained.

Fear of Misuse of Data

Some organizations resist the idea of administering surveys to their employees due to past misuse of survey data (for example, no feedback on survey results, no change as a result of the assessment, poor control of information, breaches of confidentiality). One of the best ways to undermine a change effort is to set up false expectations or betray a promise of confidentiality. Therefore, decide ahead of time what will be done with survey data. If feedback is not going to be provided or the data is not going to be held in confidence, make sure survey participants are told in advance so that no one is surprised by what is or is not done with the information.

Unskilled Survey Administrators

Unskilled survey administrators are a very common problem. Administering surveys can be difficult and takes special skills and experience. In many cases, surveys fail because the administrators did not have appropriate training. Those conducting the Change Readiness Assessment should have the following skills:

- Facilitation experience.

- A deep understanding of the eight steps.

- The ability to apply the eight steps to action plans.

- A capacity for data analysis.

- Excellent written and verbal communication skills.

- A basic understanding of how business change is implemented.

Gauging Change Readiness

It is important to remember that threats are inherent in any organizational transformation, and that risks increase exponentially as the size, complexity, and length of a change effort increase. However, risk taking is essential to the effort's progress and success. The inevitability of threats only increases the need to manage them and to minimize their consequences. With the Change Readiness Assessment, areas that threaten success can be regularly and effectively identified, making risk management straightforward and attainable.

As you progress through the transformation, different steps will become more or less risk prone, so it is necessary to regularly monitor the change horizon for threats. For example, if you have just completed a vision statement and are in the process of communicating that vision, steps 1 through 4 may be prone to threats but steps 5 through 8 may not yet be affected. If you are communicating the vision, you are mainly concerned with preparing the organization for change as opposed to implementing and sustaining the change. Therefore, the last four steps would not figure in the Change Readiness Assessment at this point. However, as the transformation continues, steps 5 through 8 will take on greater importance and you may need to circle back to earlier phases in order to address issues like urgency or communication. Remember, the eight steps are dynamic, not strictly sequential.

Deploy your Change Readiness Assessment when first creating the climate for change. Deliver assessment results to the teams guiding the change to help them develop such preliminary elements as a communication strategy and plan, leadership alignment actions, the approach for roll-out, or concrete ideas for dealing with resistance. The assessment results contribute to these deliverables by providing information about the extent of change required, what should be leveraged, and change challenges likely to require attention and action. The results are intended to provide a solid foundation to guide future activities over the life of the project.

The Change Readiness Assessment also figures into other areas of the transformation. For instance, early in the change effort the team guiding the change design may use the assessment results to better address change barriers and take advantage of uncovered opportunities. For example, in a healthcare setting, if the results suggest that physicians are uneasy about the change initiative and unsure that their needs will be considered, the guiding team might design and roll out several early, physician-specific short-term wins to help allay their fears. Or, one of the guiding teams may decide to add one or more influential physicians to the team.

How to Use the Change Readiness Assessment

- Distribute your customized Change Readiness Assessment to groups of individuals in the following four stakeholder groups:

    1. Executives and sponsors: Leaders responsible for the change effort, as well as senior executives within the organization.

    2. Managers and supervisors.

    3. Employees who will be affected by the change initiative.

    4. Project teams: Individuals assigned to the project teams that are driving the effort at the departmental levels.

- Ask the individuals being surveyed to answer the questions according to their own experiences and knowledge of the organization.

- As indicated in the directions that accompany the survey, respondents will assign a rating of 1 to 6 to each question, with 1 indicating "strongly disagree" and 6 indicating "strongly agree."

- After the sheets have been returned to you, tally the results by each of the eight areas. The farther the results are from the maximum score of 60 for each area, the more significant the threat of problems.

- After you have identified threat areas within your change effort, use the ideas and suggestions provided in this guide.

Important Tips on Using the Survey

The following tips will assist you in getting the best information as a result of using the survey. They are based on lessons learned in client settings.

- For reasons of practicality, time, or specific needs, you may want to customize the survey to better reflect your particular change effort or expand certain items into questions for focus groups. Typically, the greatest response rate with surveys of this nature occurs when they contain no more than twenty to twenty-five questions.

- The Change Readiness Assessment can be distributed as a survey or conducted as an interview/focus session in order to get more follow-up information from the respondents.

- If you do use this tool in an interview/focus group format:

  ✓ Select facilitators based on their expertise in one or several functional or technical areas that will be impacted by the change effort. Also, make sure that the facilitator can remain impartial.

  ✓ Have facilitators ask questions to prompt a better understanding of the statements in the survey. They should use open-ended questions, general comments, and recommendations to encourage open and helpful feedback.

  ✓ Have participants read the statements and questions before the session, so they'll be better prepared to respond thoughtfully.

  ✓ Encourage participants to bring documentation that pertains to their area in case they need to reference specific material to better answer a question during the session.

Reporting Change Readiness Assessment Results

After conducting the Change Readiness Assessment, it is important to compile and report on the results. Leaders often need to see and hear what the workforce is saying and thinking in order to understand what action is required. In addition, the workforce needs to see that leadership is listening to them and addressing their concerns. Depending on the size, complexity, and length of the transformation, your Change Readiness Report may include these topics:

- *Demographics:* Information on the groups to whom the survey was sent (geographic areas, levels, functions/departments) and the percentage of respondents.

- *Approach and methodology:* Details about the types of questions asked, the format used to ask the questions, and how the results were interpreted.

- *Findings:* Detailed explanation and interpretation of individual responses as well as trends expressed by stakeholder groups.

- *Summary and recommendations:* Summary of the survey responses and recommendations based on those results.

- *Next steps:* Description of what the team's next steps are now that the survey is complete. This section could include further analysis of key stakeholder perceptions and creation of the communication and change leadership strategy and plan.

It's sad but true: Often, survey data is shelved and organizations never take advantage of the valuable information provided by stakeholders. Or the data is used, but the results and actions are not shared with the stakeholders and an opportunity for a short-term win is lost.

To analyze and interpret the data, you must first organize it into a spreadsheet or database. Figure 9-1 offers a sample summary page from a Change Readiness Report (only 6 of the 8 steps were surveyed in this report). This summary represents the opinions of middle managers across all locations of a particular organization. (A summary might also include multiple organizational levels.) You may also find it beneficial to analyze data independently for a single loca-

FIGURE 9-1

Sense of urgency survey
Change readiness report: middle managers

Number of participants		Section summary	
Location 1:	6	Increase urgency	5.31
Location 2:	3	Build guiding teams	4.64
Location 3:	3	Communicate for buy-in	4.11
Location 4:	5	Enable action	4.50
Location 5:	9	Don't let up	4.67
Location 6:	6	Make change stick	4.70
Total	**32**		

Scale: 1 = Strongly disagree; 2 = Disagree; 3 = Slightly disagree; 4 = Slightly agree; 5 = Agree; 6 = Strongly agree

What specific behavior changes have you noticed in your location?

- More frequent coaching sessions.
- Our managers are interacting with us more and taking a hands-on approach for preparing us for our new roles.
- More open and honest communication/information sharing.
- Our managers are collaborating more with each other.
- Increased teamwork/collaboration.
- Our managers seen to be observing our day-to-day performance more.
- Some of our managers appear to be nervous, leading us to believe they are fearful for their own jobs.

What specific behavior changes still need to be made in your location?

- Improved communications—we never know where to look for new information.
- Our managers need to empower us to do our job by giving us the authority to make key decisions.
- Our managers need to do what they are telling us to do.
- Many of the things we still have to do aren't consistent with the vision for the future.
- We need to spend more time with the front-line employees.
- Our managers need to give up the control and let us do our jobs.
- Our managers need to be more consistent.
- Our managers need to show us that they trust us.

tion, business unit, and so forth to determine if specific barriers or threats exist. Once all threats and barriers are determined, specific action steps can be crafted.

Although the Change Readiness Report in figure 9-1 highlights middle management, it is often appropriate to distribute the assessment to a population that samples all levels of the organization. However, raising leadership's awareness of the difference between employees at various levels is often a significant challenge since leadership does not typically have the time or appetite for viewing lengthy documents. Figure 9-2, the risk wheel, helps solve this issue by visually displaying varying perceptions of a change initiative by level. I have found the risk wheel to be a very effective tool to command leadership's attention by communicating, in a very simple format, the issues the change effort faces. Once leaders acknowledge the issues, they are much more open to listening to the details of the problems and the potential actions that should be taken to resolve them.

Leaders and project team members can be tempted to believe that everyone else in the organization feels and thinks about the transformation the same way they do. Because project teams and often lead-

FIGURE 9-2

Risk wheel

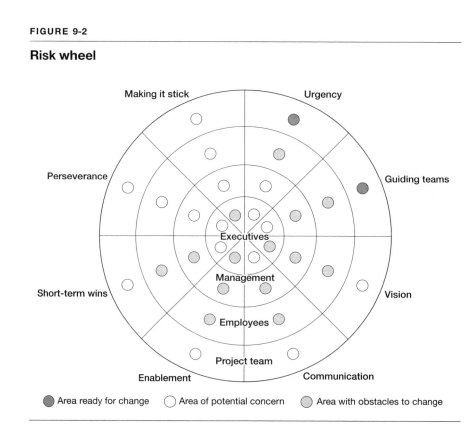

ers work toward achieving the vision on a daily basis, they have a greater understanding of the change initiative and typically are the first ones to buy into the vision. When people have already accepted a change, they often assume that others share their view and lose patience with those who do not demonstrate attitude and behavior changes consistent with the vision. The risk wheel can quickly bring leaders and project team members back to reality by highlighting differences among various groups.

Final Thoughts

The goal of this *Field Guide* has been to provide individuals who want to use the eight-step approach with a set of usable and practical suggestions, tools, and templates that have been field tested and proven to work. However, the key to success in any change effort does not reside in the tools or templates but rather in the desire of those leading the initiative to succeed. Without this desire, which is manifested as a feeling of urgency, the change effort will run out of gas.

Simply put, without urgency and the emotion and energy it produces, the efforts to align guiding teams, get the vision right, communicate the vision, and enable the organization to make the change have little chance of being effective. If the initial steps are not properly set as the foundation on which the change is built, it is impossible for the last two steps—don't let up and make it stick—to be effective. If those individuals who are driving the change are not demonstrating their full commitment to the change, their messages will have very limited impact and the initiative is unlikely to succeed. Successfully transforming any organization is hard work even when leadership is fully behind the effort—it is near impossible if leadership does not lead the effort.

Since writing *The Heart of Change* with John Kotter, I have met with thousands of people around the world, in both the private and public sectors, to discuss the eight steps and the critical part emotion and energy play in successful change. Every time I speak to groups I ask the participants the following question:

Think back to the moment you realized that a change effort you were working on was a success. At that moment, were you thinking about some fact or figure, or were you feeling something like joy, pride, excitement?

What do you think is the response? Almost invariably, people say they were feeling emotion and energy. This is the lifeblood—the heart—of change. So, to be successful with your change effort, you must build the necessary level of energy and urgency, and then be sure your passion spreads like a virus. Only then can you have the tenacity needed to make the change stick.

The *Field Guide* has taken the eight steps and the stories described in *Leading Change* and *The Heart of Change* one step further. It provides the infrastructure to put the eight steps into action in your organization. By using the *Field Guide* you can now determine if you have a sufficient level of energy to initiate a change effort. In addition, you have an integrated tool set to develop a communication program founded on heartfelt, simple, and candid messages. Moreover, you now have not only the ability to identify short-term wins but also the tools to implement and track them to completion. Finally, by having a deeper understanding of the eight steps, you are now in a position to take this change framework and use it across your entire organization whenever a change is taking place.

Think about it—a framework whereby everyone in your organization understands the change and sees the benefits of the outcome. Imagine for a moment how effectively your organization could deal with change issues if everyone understood the nuances of the issues rather than having multiple groups with multiple approaches. Imagine if everyone spoke the same "change language" and, rather than adapting your language and framework to the latest consultant's approach, your consultants adapted their language and framework to the eight steps. Wouldn't it be interesting if when you shared an issue related to urgency, your guiding team fully understood the implications and, furthermore, had their own sense of urgency to take the appropriate action? This would be powerful, and this is where the *Field Guide* can help. Use the tools, templates, and suggestions to customize the framework and the steps to the needs of your organization. Be bold; create new templates and diagnostics. Think about who needs what level of understanding about the eight steps, and develop your own stories that enable people to see the need for change—stories that describe what happened when the workforce faced barriers, or how one of your initiatives failed to live up to expectations because success was declared prematurely, or how a change succeeded because people's efforts were recognized and rewarded. Change is hard work. Having a framework that helps people see and feel the need for the change increases your probability of success.

INDEX

Dan S. Cohen is a Principal with Deloitte Consulting LLC where he focuses his consulting activities on large-scale organizational transformation. He heads Deloitte Consulting's Global Energy Change Leadership practice and led the development of the firm's Global Change Leadership Methodology. He has provided consulting support to a number of *Fortune* 100 companies such as Exxon-Mobil, Baker Hughes, Dell, The Coca-Cola Company, and Reliant Energy. Prior to consulting, he worked in the manufacturing, financial, and real estate industries for over fifteen years in various executive human resource positions. In addition to his consulting work, Cohen has lectured on organizational behavior at the University of Detroit, Ohio State University, Miami University, and Southern Methodist University. He obtained his BA at Adelphi University, his MA at the University of Detroit, and his PhD at Ohio State.

Cohen lives in Plano, Texas, with his wife Ronnie. He can be reached at dacohen@dc.com.